CASE STUDIES IN
JAPANESE NEGOTIATING BEHAVIOR

Case Studies in Japanese Negotiating Behavior

Michael Blaker, Paul Giarra, and Ezra F. Vogel

UNITED STATES INSTITUTE OF PEACE PRESS
Washington, D.C.

UNITED STATES INSTITUTE OF PEACE
1200 17th Street NW
Washington, DC 20036

© 2002 by the Endowment of the United States Institute of Peace.

First published 2002

Printed in the United States of America

The paper used in this publication meets the minimum requirements of American National Standards for Information Science—Permanence of Paper for Printed Library Materials, ANSI Z39.48-1984.

Library of Congress Cataloging-in-Publication Data
Blaker, Michael, 1940-
   Case studies in Japanese negotiating behavior / Michael Blaker, Paul Giarra, and Ezra Vogel.
      p. cm.
   Includes bibliographical references.
   ISBN 1-929223-10-2
      1. Negotiation in business–Japan–Case studies. 2. Negotiation–Japan–Psychological aspects–Case studies. 3. Negotiation–United States–Psychological aspects –Case studies. 4. Diplomacy. 5. Japan–Commercial treaties–United States–Case studies. 6. United States–Commercial treaties–Case studies. 7. Japan–Foreign relations–United States–Case studies. 8. United States–Foreign relations–Japan– Case studies. I. Giarra, Paul, 1949- II. Vogel, Ezra F. III. Title.

HD58.6 .56 2002
382'.952073–dc21
                                                                    2002031967

CONTENTS

CASE STUDIES IN
JAPANESE NEGOTIATING BEHAVIOR

INTRODUCTION

In his classic work *Diplomacy*, Sir Harold Nicolson identified four national styles of diplomatic negotiation: Warrior, Machiavellian, Manipulative, and Compromising.[1] The bargaining styles of the Americans, the Russians, the Chinese, and the British, respectively, may seem to fit into Nicolson's four categories. But what of the Japanese? To which group would they belong? One Japanese diplomat, after reflecting on Nicolson's typology, concluded that Japanese negotiating behavior could not be placed into any of the four groups. When asked why not, he dryly replied, "Because Japan has no style in the first place!"

Is there any truth to such a claim? Have the Japanese somehow managed to evolve a negotiating style that defies categorization because—unlike, say, Russian or Chinese diplomacy—it exhibits no distinctive characteristics? Alternatively, can Japan be said to have no style of its own because its diplomats—acculturated into a transnational elite who embrace Western norms and modes of thought, dress, and behavior—act no differently than the diplomats of other Western nations?

To these questions, this volume offers an unambiguous answer: no. In the following chapters, we examine four diplomatic encounters between Japan and the United States over the past twenty-five years. Two of our cases center on U.S. access to Japanese markets for agricultural products. The other two focus on security issues; one involves Japanese proposals to develop a new fighter aircraft, the other examines efforts to refashion the U.S.-Japanese security relationship in the 1990s. In each case, distinctive patterns can be seen in the approach and behavior of the Japanese negotiators. Moreover, as our concluding chapter makes clear, those patterns are replicated, to a greater or lesser extent, across the four cases.

This finding, we should note, would not surprise the majority of practitioners and scholars of international negotiation. Most experts agree that national diplomatic styles differ. While particular moves are not unique to any country, the mix of tactics employed by diplomats from a given nation adds up to a distinctive composite portrait of that nation's style. This volume, indeed, is part of a broader project designed to facilitate international communication by identifying and analyzing such differences in national negotiating styles. Sponsored by the United States Institute of Peace, the cross-cultural negotiation project has already yielded book-length studies of Chinese, Russian, North Korean, and German negotiating behavior; an analysis of French behavior is also under way.[2] *Case Studies in Japanese Negotiating Behavior* is less ambitious than most of those studies insofar as it focuses on a limited number of case studies rather than on portraying the full range of its subject's motivation, style, and conduct. Nonetheless, if this is more a sketch than a definitive portrait, the lines of the drawing are clear enough.

DESCRIBING JAPANESE NEGOTIATING BEHAVIOR

Most of the literature on negotiating with Japan falls into the category of "how-to" manuals for conducting business-level negotiations. The Japanese *diplomatic* style has attracted far less attention from non-Japanese writers, although a few general works and a dozen or so studies of single issues are available.[3] Most Japanese-authored accounts that claim to address negotiations really deal with foreign policy or diplomacy. Of the works that discuss negotiating conduct, virtually all are blow-by-blow chronologies of bilateral (typically Japanese-American) interactions on single issues. Only a handful of Japanese analysts have examined Japan's approach toward and management of the negotiating process itself, including an assessment of the pros and cons of alternative bargaining moves, strategies, and tactics.

When Japanese writers have explored the behavior of Japan's negotiators, they have assigned much weight to Japanese-style communication patterns, sociocultural traits, and psychological characteristics. Widely cited examples include seeking harmony *(wa)*, expecting to be looked after *(amae)*, taking a stance on reading the opponent *(haragei)*, balancing the surface *(omote)* and the behind-the-scenes *(ura)*, concern for face *(mentsu)*, instinctive communication *(ishin denshin)*, and building consensus before moving *(nemawashi)*. To Japanese authors, these attributes not only impart an identifiable Japanese flavor to the behavior but also explain why Japanese diplomats and negotiators have encountered so much criticism for their way of dealing with other countries across the bargaining table.

What, exactly, *is* Japan's way of dealing with its negotiating counterparts? The answer that emerges from our four case studies may help to explain why the Japanese diplomat quoted at the outset of this chapter denied the existence of a Japanese style. Perhaps he was merely being mischievous. Perhaps, however, he was reflecting, albeit obliquely, the unease with which the Japanese have tended to approach international negotiation, an unease that has produced a negotiating style that is more cautious and more reactive, less demonstrative and less visible, than that of other powerful nations.

Most Japanese today would no doubt agree with a remark made by Toshimichi Okubo over a century ago. "Dealing with foreigners," the Meiji-era statesman observed, "can be a troublesome and difficult task." Ever since 1853, when Commodore Matthew Perry's "black ships" sailed into Edo Bay, piercing the curtain of Japan's centuries of virtual isolation from the outside world, the Japanese people and their leaders have regarded diplomacy and diplomatic negotiations as formidable, face-threatening undertakings. As the first three of our cases show, even during the Cold War, when Japan emerged as an important strategic ally of the United States and a powerhouse of the global economy, Japan usually approached the negotiating table warily, especially when its negotiating counterpart was the United States and especially when the subject for discussion was trade. Since the end of the Cold War (as our fourth case reveals), some Japanese diplomats have displayed signs of a new, more self-confident, demeanor, which has contributed to more cooperative and productive relationships with their opposite numbers. Even so, much of this new-found assertiveness seems superficial; underneath, one suspects, the same wariness and unease remain.

This characterization of Japan's approach to diplomatic negotiations might seem dubious to American businesspeople and trade representatives who spent frustrating and often fruitless years wrestling with obstinate and sometimes aggressive Japanese negotiators for access to Japan's domestic markets in the 1970s, 1980s, and 1990s. Such Americans might well paraphrase Okubo's remark to read, "Dealing with *Japanese* can be a troublesome and difficult task." Indeed it can—but two qualifications need to be made. First, in Japanese-U.S. negotiations over the past thirty years, trade issues have generally excited much more rancor and contention than have strategic and security issues—a point that comes out clearly in the fourth of our case studies. Second, many of the traits that U.S. trade negotiators have found most galling in their Japanese counterparts—for instance, a snail-like pace and an obsessive attention to detail—are products of, not aberrations from, an underlying cautiousness and defensiveness.

According to Michael Blaker, author of the first three of our case studies, a good label for the behavior of Japanese negotiators is "coping," an attitude that is consistently evident both at the loftier plateau of diplomacy and down in the trenches at the level of direct negotiations. Coping captures the go-with-the-flow essence of the Japanese bargaining approach: testing the waters through a process of consultations, discussions, information gathering, and reconnaissance; cautiously appraising the external situation; methodically weighing and sorting each and every option; deferring action on contentious issues; crafting a domestic consensus on the situation faced; making minimal adjustments or concessions to block, circumvent, or dissolve criticism; and adapting to a situation with minimal risk.

Japan, Blaker argues, typically prefers to avoid negotiating with the United States. When Japan is forced to do so, it then seeks to minimize the scope of the issues at stake. This issue-avoidance and issue-minimization behavior springs in part from Japan's self-image as a vulnerable island state with few natural advantages and always in danger of being isolated internationally. In part, too, it arises from recognition of the fact that in negotiations with the United States, Japan tends to give up far more than it gets. Blaker traces a recurrent pattern in which Japanese negotiators, faced with U.S. demands, first insist on the inflexibility of Japan's position and seek to wear down the U.S. side's resolve; gradually, however, Japan makes a series of concessions, each of its compromises being rationalized as the least-worst option available and as necessary to prevent Japan's isolation.

In their case study, Ezra Vogel and Paul Giarra paint a picture of Japanese behavior that seems at first quite different. Their account of the Nye initiative undertaken in the mid-1990s to refashion the U.S.-Japanese security relationship tells of a remarkable level of mutual understanding achieved through close and frequent consultation among diplomats and policymakers on both sides. Discussions proceeded relatively smoothly and speedily, and within just a few years an agreement was signed that reflected the post–Cold War environment and promised a larger role for Japan in regional security.

Yet, while the pace and cooperative tenor of these negotiations stand in stark contrast to the cases analyzed by Blaker, similarities can be found. For instance, as in the bargaining over imports of rice and oranges and development of the FSX aircraft, so in the security negotiations of the mid-1990s progress toward agreement hinged on creating a favorable consensus within the Japanese bureaucracy. Indeed, Vogel and Giarra, who were themselves key players in the initiative, emphasize the vital importance of securing support from a broad array of groups.

Moreover, the negotiations of the mid-1990s were to a large extent atypical of U.S.-Japanese encounters on security matters. Much more typical was the kind of behavior described in the other case studies. Prior to the Nye initiative, U.S.-Japanese relations on security and military issues had been manageable but highly constrained and marked by mutual dissatisfaction. The American side had long been frustrated by Japan's refusal to shoulder more of the burden of its own defense and to make more explicit commitments to supporting U.S. military operations in a regional crisis. For their part, the Japanese feared being abandoned by the United States at a critical moment, had political misgivings about assuming a more active military role, and sought to avoid entangling arrangements that would lead to a loss of national prerogatives. In a manner very similar to the pattern of issue avoidance and issue minimization that Blaker describes, Japan, wary of U.S. motives, reflexively resisted American attempts to broaden the security relationship. This attitude changed significantly but only temporarily during the Nye initiative. Almost immediately after the signing in April 1996 of the Japan-U.S. Joint Declaration on Security Alliance for the Twenty-First Century, the cooperation and consultation that had begun to blossom began to wither. Once the initiative's leading sponsors departed Washington, high-level U.S. officials paid little attention to Japanese security matters, leaving Tokyo to contemplate forging a more independent role for itself on the international stage.

To a large extent, the Nye initiative was the exception that proved the rule about Japanese negotiating behavior vis-à-vis the United States. Wary of U.S. ambitions and conscious of its own relative weakness, Japan has preferred to avoid or minimize negotiations. When it has accepted that it must negotiate, it has tended to do so cautiously, methodically, and slowly and has signed an agreement only after crafting a broad internal consensus and persuading itself that the agreement is the least-worst option available. This pattern *may* be changing, not least because of the advent of a generation of younger officials who are readier to cooperate and pursue constructive, mutually beneficial solutions. Any such change, however, is likely to be piecemeal and gradual.

EXPLAINING JAPANESE NEGOTIATING BEHAVIOR

Where do these behavioral traits and characteristic approaches come from? This book is much too short for us to embark on a comprehensive exploration of the origins of Japanese negotiating behavior. However, the behavior of Japanese negotiators described in the following chapters may be more comprehensible if we outline, albeit briefly, three factors whose interplay shapes much of the Japanese bargaining style. Those factors are culture; domestic institutions and political processes; and Japan's subordinate position in the U.S.-Japan relationship.

Culture

Culture—in the sense of a "complex system of meanings created, shared, and transmitted (socially inherited) by individuals in particular social groups"[4]—undoubtedly plays a role in molding the uniquely Japanese brand of negotiating conduct. In particular, beliefs about and perceptions of the outside world, and values and norms concerning social relationships, exercise a powerful influence.

The Japanese tend to display a "fortress mentality," regarding their island country as surrounded and vulnerable but also as distinct, separate, and in many ways superior. This attitude is expressed through various powerful ideas and concepts that pervade the language and culture. It can be seen, for example, in paired terms such as *uchi* (inside, we) and *soto* (foreign, them), and *honne* (innermost feelings, as expressed to other

Japanese) and *tatemae* (verbal or superficial expression, as embodied in official statements). This outlook helps to explain why Japanese negotiators often display an uneasiness toward and suspicion of the outside world, an ultrasensitivity to foreign opinions and criticisms, and a near-obsessive concern with Japan's weakness and vulnerability. This unease is tempered to some degree in relationships that Japan regards as fundamentally positive; in such relationships, Japanese negotiators feel sufficiently confident to make a series of small adjustments in order to reach a consensus with their negotiating partners. However, where Japanese negotiators feel that there is not a basically good relationship, they can become very stubborn.

Within Japanese society, it has traditionally been the case that the individual is seen as subordinate to the group to which he or she belongs, be it the family, extended family, corporation, or government ministry. Society is very hierarchical; everyone has a well-defined position and role, and dissension and outspokenness are strongly discouraged. The individual is seen as potentially disruptive of a highly prized concept—*wa* (harmony). Being assertive and inventive, taking risks and initiatives: these tend not to be actions that are rewarded within Japanese society. (The Japanese, it may be noted, do not have their own word for "initiative"—or for "give-and-take" or "partnership"—but they have fifty words that mean, more or less, "reading the situation.") The effect of these attitudes is evident at the negotiating table, where Japanese diplomats rarely make bold moves or propose new initiatives, and where a change in the personnel of the Japanese delegation rarely alters the complexion or dynamic of the discussions.

Yet, while Japan is a stratified society, that does not make it a tranquil society. To the contrary, it is in many ways fragmented and pluralistic. It is, to be sure, a vertically organized society, but it is also structured horizontally—and at each level there are numerous groups (almost independent domains) fiercely assertive of their own interests and locked in competition with one another. The Japanese have to take these separate elements and combine them in a mutually accommodative way; decisions are thus not so much reached by a logical analysis of options as arranged by the interests and relative power of the various actors. Effective Japanese leaders are consensus builders, able to figure out how to accommodate the interests of each group or to compensate those groups whose interests are harmed by an agreement. In part because of this, negotiation is not seen as a legitimate clash of different points of view but as a failure of the consensus process. International negotiation is to some extent not negotiation at all but an attempt to carry out the domestic agreements reached by a consensus-building process. Negotiation represents, in Japanese eyes, a failure on the Japanese part to communicate their point of view, which if communicated would have been understood as valid and accepted by the negotiating counterpart. If an impasse occurs, it is attributed to the failure of Japan's diplomats to explain to the other side Japan's position and the constraints under which it is laboring. Hence, we see such bizarre aspects of Japanese negotiating behavior as rounds of delegations coming from Japan to hurl themselves against foreign resistance, convinced that they have just to convey the Japanese point of view in order to reach a mutually acceptable agreement.

Some cultural influences exert a distinctly visible and audible (or conspicuously inaudible) impact on negotiations. The Japanese cultural disinclination to utter an outright "No" and the inclination to smile and nod to indicate understanding, but not necessarily agreement, have often misled Western negotiators. So, too, has the Japanese use of silence. Silence is perfectly acceptable in Japanese social interactions. Indeed, it is expected of senior officials and respected elders. Non-Japanese, however, tend to misinterpret Japanese silence in the face of a counterpart's proposal as signaling agreement or at least acquiescence. As UN undersecretary general Yasushi Akashi remarked, Japanese diplomats have "big ears and small mouths."[5] Body language is another element of Japanese negotiating behavior whose significance and meaning have often been overlooked. The art of taking a physical stance and reading the opponent (*haragei*, literally, "stomach art") is refined and eloquent and is used chiefly for communication among Japanese.

Domestic Institutions and Political Processes

As noted, Japan is a highly pluralistic society. Reaching public policy decisions is an intensely combative, heavily bureaucratic, consensus-driven process of accommodating diverse interests and viewpoints. The executive has very limited ability to impose its decisions on government bureaucracies, which tend to be extremely powerful entities, each a disciplined hierarchy within itself and fiercely competitive with other ministries or agencies for the dominance of its viewpoint. Various interest groups, the politicians who represent them, and the policy *zoku*, or "tribes" (issue-specific cadres of Diet members), also shoulder their way into the decision-making process. All bureaucratic, democratic societies face similar difficulties. But what distinguishes Japan is the utter complexity of the domestic consensus-building process.

The need to reach consensus means that Japan is slow to develop a negotiating position and is severely constrained from departing from it during negotiations. It enters negotiations with very little room for maneuver, which largely rules out the use of trade-offs, bluffs, and Machiavellian tactics. Anticipatory concessions have already been made at home, in the process of reaching a consensus on an initial negotiating position. Thus, when confronted with demands for concessions at negotiations, the Japanese may say, in effect, "We already did that!" When the other side presents a new proposal or raises new issues, the Japanese negotiating team cannot offer any substantive response until a new domestic consensus has been forged.

Furthermore, the Japanese government is structured in such a way that negotiating responsibility rests on a foreign ministry that serves a largely coordinating role, or on negotiators who represent parochial, narrow interests with little independent power, even as they officially are assigned responsibility to reflect the hopes, interests, and values of the nation as a whole. In other words, the negotiating team is essentially a representative for the domestic coalition that has been forged. One consequence is that delegations are often large, unwieldy, and even disunited, with representatives of the different domestic groups refusing to share information with one another. Another casualty of bureaucratic parochialism is that the negotiating process channel is poorly linked to the negotiating policy channel. Only a political crisis activates the process sufficiently to engage the top Japanese leaders who can work out the last-minute compromises among domestic players to permit a final settlement to be reached.

Japan's Subordinate Position

A third factor exerts a strong influence on Japanese bargaining behavior toward the United States; this factor, not surprisingly, is Japan's relationship with the United States. It is a relationship that since Japanese independence in 1952 has been decidedly asymmetrical. The "strategic bargain"—an unstated bargain, it should be noted—then struck essentially meant that Japan would allow the Americans to shelter it under the U.S. security umbrella and would give up some of its self-respect and sovereignty in exchange for U.S. help in rebuilding and developing its economy and access to the U.S. market. For the United States, the strategic bargain was attractive because it effectively precluded the reemergence of a militaristic and aggressive Japan, hostile to U.S. influence in the region; instead, Japan would be a base for U.S. power in Southeast Asia.

As a consequence, Japan has been willing to defer to the United States, especially on security and strategic issues, though it has expected the United States to recognize and respect Japanese interests and sensitivities. At the highest political levels, Japanese leaders have also been wary of resisting U.S. trade demands too forcibly, fearful of alienating U.S. support and imperiling the security relationship. The U.S. agenda has been —by dint of Japan's deference and hesitancy about introducing its own initiatives—Japan's agenda.

However, although the basic security relationship has endured, it has certainly undergone shifts in character. During the Occupation of 1945–52, the Japanese felt they had no choice but to be compliant with the U.S. authorities, but they created some leverage by adopting the classic strategy of the underdog in a tight-knit society: when faced with an unpalatable order from the occupying power, the Japanese would purposely misunderstand, raise innumerable practical objections, and repeatedly delay action. From the mid-1950s until 1972 (with one very brief exception), all Japanese prime ministers came from the so-called Yoshida school, which was named after the Liberal Democratic Party (LDP) prime minister who held office for most of the period from 1947 to 1955. The Yoshida school recruited talented former bureaucrats and trained them into a cadre of young and highly talented politicians with a disciplined commitment to overall national goals that had traditionally been found in the bureaucracy. These LDP leaders recognized the need to work with the United States for the security alliance and were thus prepared to push through the security treaty agreements in 1959–60 and 1969 despite great public opposition in Japan.

Well into the 1970s, most Japanese dealings with other countries were handled by the Ministry of Foreign Affairs. Ministry officials learned to adapt to the United States and worked closely with U.S. State Department officials, developing relationships of trust and understanding. They felt comfortable in dealing within this context, much in line with the traditional Japanese pattern of working with trusted partners to resolve issues. However, as relations with foreign countries continued to expand, more branches of government had to increase their direct contacts with other countries. At first some of these relationships were awkward, but gradually various ministries acquired expertise. Furthermore, from the 1970s into the mid-1990s, relations between Japan and the United States were strained by a succession of trade wars. As disagreements and ill feelings multiplied, those officials on both sides who had established close and cooperative relationships with their counterparts came under suspicion for being too willing to make concessions. During the Cold War, the White House and the Department of Defense had sought to restrain U.S. trade negotiators from pushing the Japanese too hard, fearing the consequences for national security. But with the end of the Cold War, the U.S. government saw less reason to restrain its negotiators. Soon, even top-level political encounters could no longer be guaranteed to yield a compromise agreement.

The origins of these trade wars can be found in the economic and trade strategies Japan adopted early in the Cold War. As described in chapter 1 (see p. 18), Japan embraced the so-called Yoshida doctrine of separating politics from economics (*seikei bunri* in Japanese), and Japanese leaders were willing to bend to satisfy American security goals as long as Japanese economic development was not threatened. Japanese economic strategy emphasized the importance of importing as few industrial products as possible in order to build up Japan's own industries and to maintain a positive trade balance to pay for the resources and the food that Japan must import. Japan also sought to protect its agricultural sector, which had powerful political support, from foreign competition. Japanese exporters focused their attention on the large U.S. market—indeed, Japan was heavily dependent on that market until the Asian markets began to develop in the 1980s and 1990s.

At first, the United States viewed Japanese protectionism with equanimity, but once Japanese industries (in areas such as textiles, steel, consumer electronics, and automobiles) began to claim a significant and increasing share of the U.S. market, U.S. companies pressed for barriers to Japanese imports and for greater access to the Japanese market. Although the Japanese government was careful not to imperil its security relationship with the United States, it resisted U.S. demands and was slow to open its markets. As noted above, the result was a succession of trade wars that ran from the 1970s into the 1990s.

Fortunately, as the 1990s advanced, relations began to improve. The establishment of the World Trade Organization and the gradual multilateralization of trade agreements prompted many Japanese to proclaim the end of the era of bilateral trade wars. At much the same time, an economic downturn in Japan prompted an opening of the Japanese financial markets, which in turn greatly reduced pressure from the American side. Furthermore, as detailed in chapter 4, the two countries adjusted their security relationship to reflect the changed conditions of the post–Cold War environment and to guard against instability in the region. The negotiations over this new security framework were conducted in a remarkably cordial and cooperative atmosphere. Subsequently, however, progress toward closer military cooperation has faltered.

Since the end of the Cold War, many observers claim to see signs of a more self-confident Japan. They point to a group of younger Japanese diplomats, who seem more at ease in international forums than did their predecessors, and more inclined to develop an independent role for Japan in the region and the world at large. Japan is indeed showing greater independence, but it is a very gradual process. The Japanese today are reevaluating the strategic bargain struck fifty years ago, but they do not seem to have arrived at any far-reaching conclusions. Even when pressured by other countries—including the United States—to play a more active role on the international stage, Japan has usually shown a marked reluctance to assume new responsibilities. Perhaps, however, such trepidation is finally eroding. In the aftermath of the terrorist attacks on the World Trade Center and the Pentagon on September 11, 2001, the government of Junichiro Koizumi announced plans to back up the international effort to combat terrorism. To facilitate these measures, it submitted an antiterrorism bill and a proposed amendment to the Self-Defense Forces Law to the Diet.

Within the context of the U.S.-Japanese relationship, Japan clearly remains the junior partner. Moreover, it continues to play that role in much the same manner as it has done since the 1950s: as a generally loyal, if some-times exasperated and resentful, subordinate. Unlike, say, Israel and South Korea, which are no less dependent on the United States, Japan has rarely sought to act in defiance of U.S. wishes or to manipulate the United States for its own ends. Instead, the fundamentally reactive, defensive, and cau-tious nature of Japanese negotiating behavior has been accentuated in encounters with the United States. This is not to say that Japan has not sought to enhance its bargaining position whenever possible; for instance, it learned early on in the trade wars the value of working with Congress to influence negotiating outcomes and of locating Japanese industries in many U.S. states. Even so, rather than advancing their own agenda, Japanese diplomats have sought to anticipate U.S. demands, to moderate them, and then to satisfy them, albeit at the lowest cost to Japan.

CAVEATS AND CASES

Does Japan display the same negotiating behavior in encounters with coun-tries other than the United States? Unfortunately, this question must be left to future studies. This volume focuses squarely on bilateral U.S.-Japanese negotiations. We caution against applying our analyses and conclusions auto-matically to other bilateral relationships or even to multilateral forums involving other countries as well as Japan and the United States. This is not to say that we would expect to find an entirely different Japanese bargaining style in negotiations involving other major powers. It seems likely that even in negotiations between Japan and middle-ranking and smaller powers, the cultural, institutional, and political factors outlined above would exert a similar influence on Japanese conduct. Nonetheless, we emphasize that our findings relate only to encounters between Japan and the United States.

We should also stress that our cases by no means exhaust the variety of subjects that have exercised the diplomatic skills of the two countries. For example, we do not cover the high-profile, highly charged struggles over issues such as textiles, automobiles, steel, and semiconductors. Nor do we cover bargaining from the standpoint of business negotiators. Certainly, we note the involvement, direct and indirect, of corporations from both countries in official negotiations (and in the case of Japan especially, the line between the public and the private sectors can be extremely fuzzy), but our focus throughout is on governmental, not corporate, negotiators. Thus, we do not discuss, for instance, questions as to whether Japanese corporate negotiators launch more initiatives and take greater risks than their diplomatic colleagues (they almost certainly do) or whether corporate culture can reflect variant streams of Japanese culture.

With these caveats in mind, however, we trust that readers will find our four cases illuminating. They range across much of the past twenty-five years—and thus reflect the vicissitudes in Japanese-U.S. relations during that period. They deal not only with trade issues but also with security matters—and thus allow comparisons to be drawn between Japanese behavior in those two fields. And they cover negotiations that yielded mutually rewarding outcomes as well as encounters that left one or both parties feeling aggrieved and defeated—and thus they counter simplistic but not uncommon stereotypes that paint one or the other side as omniscient and omnipotent.

Furthermore, our authors provide complementary perspectives on the events they describe. Michael Blaker offers a scholar's perspective, one informed by extensive reading of Japanese sources, interviews with influential U.S. and Japanese negotiators, and his expert knowledge of the history of U.S.-Japanese negotiations. Ezra Vogel and Paul Giarra give us an insider's account of one such set of negotiations. Both men were closely involved with the effort to develop a new security framework for U.S.-Japanese relations in the 1990s. Professor Vogel is a Harvard academic who served as national intelligence officer for Asia from 1993 to 1995. Commander Giarra is a career navy officer specializing in Japan. Their account of those talks is authoritative and revealing.

The insights of all three authors are brought together in a concluding chapter by Patrick Cronin. Cronin—who has considerable experience in facilitating the exchange of ideas between the policymaking and scholarly communities, and who is thus perfectly suited to his task in this volume—draws out the similarities and the differences among our four case studies. Not only does he offer explanations for those variations but also he sketches out a dynamic model of Japanese negotiating behavior that puts continuity and change into perspective.

1

NEGOTIATIONS ON ORANGE IMPORTS, 1977—88

Michael Blaker

etween 1977 and 1988, the United States repeatedly pressed Japan to open its market to U.S. oranges. The two countries signed three agreements—in 1978, 1983, and 1988—each of which opened the Japanese market a little wider; and in the final agreement Japan accepted total removal of import quotas and thus complete liberalization of its market for oranges by April 1991.

This discussion concentrates on the negotiation of the first of these agreements, as Japanese behavior during bargaining on the second and third agreements was much the same.

The Japanese side's handling of these negotiations fits what might be termed the classic model of Japanese bargaining behavior on trade issues vis-à-vis the United States. The Japanese were faced with an American side that took the offensive and was willing and able to apply various forms of pressure—from advice, requests, and suggestions to threats of retaliation, sanctions, investigations, and embargoes—to persuade Japan to negotiate items on the U.S. agenda.

For its part, Japan played defense, looking first to avoid bargaining and then to minimize the scope of the negotiations. Aware of its subordinate position in its overall relationship with the United States, sensitive to foreign criticism, and fearful of international isolation, Japan accepted that final concessions were inevitable. Even so, Japanese negotiators moved slowly and Japanese policymakers publicly declared their implacable opposition to compromise, hoping to wear down the American side while buying enough time to forge (and reforge) a consensus among competing Japanese ministries, interest groups, and politicians—a consensus without which no negotiating position could be advanced and no deal agreed to.

HISTORICAL BACKGROUND

Japan's post–World War II drive to develop industries to produce goods for export was fueled in large part by the need to feed its people. With insufficient agricultural land (just 16 percent of Japan is arable) to feed a population swollen by some seven million with the return from overseas of Japanese soldiers and civilians in 1945 and with almost no natural resources of its own, Japan was reliant on manufactured exports to pay for food and natural resources. Thus, Japan developed an industrial policy that allowed the import of those foreign products essential for industry and basic resource requirements but limited the import of products that might compete with infant Japanese industries and of luxury goods that would waste Japanese funds needed to buy machinery and technology.

Japan's agricultural policy differed in that Japanese farmers were encouraged to grow food for domestic consumption, not for export. But agricultural policy mirrored industrial policy in its emphasis on strict controls of imports that would compete with homegrown agricultural products.

Throughout the 1950s and much of the 1960s, the United States and other Western countries saw little reason to challenge Japan's protectionist economic approach. In 1952, when the American Occupation of Japan ended, few Westerners could imagine that Japan would become a major industrial power within a couple of decades. The American government was prepared to be generous when Japan became a central part of the American alliance network in the Cold War–divided Asia that emerged in the 1950s. For their part, Japanese leaders quite pragmatically were prepared to bend to satisfy American security goals. They decided to accept a subordinate role for Japan in its defense and security relationship with the United States, as long as Japanese economic development was not threatened. This implicit bargain, the heart of the so-called Yoshida doctrine of separating politics from economics (*seikei bunri* in Japanese) remains the foundation of U.S.-Japanese alliance relations to this day. At the time, Japanese acceptance of the implicit deal had other advantages for a Japan still struggling to recover from the devastation of the Pacific War: it meant, in the short term, receiving vitally needed economic assistance; in the medium term, receiving technological assistance; and in the long term, gaining access to the American marketplace for Japanese manufactured products.

The contextual basis of this Japanese-American bargain began to erode during the 1960s. First, in 1964, Japan joined the Organization for Economic Cooperation and Development (OECD) and officially accepted the obligation to liberalize its economy gradually—that is, to gradually remove all import restrictions—as it grew stronger. Second, whereas until 1967 the United States had exported more to Japan than it imported, after 1967 the situation reversed. The growth of Japan's trade surplus over the succeeding years made this an increasingly sensitive issue, especially because U.S. exports in many sectors still faced import barriers in Japan. Third, the growth of Japanese textile exports in the late 1960s—and the subsequent rise in exports of Japanese consumer electronics and the expansion and upgrading of its steel, automobile, and, later, high-technology industries—created great competitive pressure on U.S. industry. American industries in turn put enormous pressure on the U.S. government to help them in their losing battle with their Japanese competitors.

In 1971, the Japanese were jolted by two high-voltage messages from Washington—messages that had profound long-term implications for relations between these erstwhile enemies and recent allies. First, Japan was hit by the ending of the Breton Woods exchange-rate system, which had pegged the Japanese yen at 360 to the U.S. dollar. Second, Tokyo was astonished to hear of the American opening to China without having been informed of it in advance by its ostensible ally, the United States. This pair of "Nixon shocks," as the Japanese describe the two electrifying events of 1971, demonstrated vividly the degree to which Japanese-U.S. ties had become highly politicized.

More important, from the standpoint of how American government officials would approach negotiations with the Japanese in the decades to follow, was the realization that the unexpected intensity of the Japanese response might be a behavioral trait that could be exploited by the purposeful application of political pressure on the Japanese. The Japanese response to the Nixon shocks seems to have convinced American officials that shock therapy could advance U.S. policy interests in negotiations with the Japanese. Successive U.S. administrations seem to have seen confirmation of this shock hypothesis in the subsequent Japanese responses to the "soybean shock" of 1973, the twin "oil shocks" of 1973 and 1979, and, rather lower on the seismic scale, an "orange shock" arising from the events covered in this chapter. (The "rice import shock" of 1990 is covered in the next chapter.) Thus was born the notion of *gaiatsu*, or "foreign pressure," as the preferred instrument for American governments in their bilateral negotiations with Japanese governments.

Both of the Nixon shocks were connected to the U.S.-Japanese wrangle over Japanese barriers to the import of U.S. textiles. By 1971, the United States and Japan had entered an era in which, while their basic security relationship remained quite manageable, their economic relations deteriorated into a series of acrimonious disputes on trade-related issues that would persist to the mid-1990s.

In 1977, the Japanese government succumbed to American pressure and agreed to bilateral negotiations on opening its domestic market to imported oranges. There was nothing new in this process, as American prodding had been behind Japan's 1964 decision to liberalize its market for imported lemons. Moreover, pressure from Washington had been responsible for Tokyo's adoption in 1971 of a quota-based system for imported grapefruit and oranges. By the mid-1970s the long American list of specific demands concerning trade had shortened, as agreements were negotiated regarding color film, computers, textiles, color TVs, and soybeans, as well as lemons and grapefruit. Some twenty-two agenda items, including oranges, remained unresolved.

U.S. insistence on orange imports as a specific agenda item surfaced in 1972–73; the Japanese side resisted, flatly turning down the American demands. However, while rejecting U.S. demands officially, Tokyo began on its own gradually to raise the quota of imported oranges to 15,000 metric tons annually.

The Japanese government might have averted American hectoring on oranges had it continued to increase these yearly amounts, but it did not. Instead, orange imports were limited to 15,000 metric tons per year until 1977, when they drew the attention of Carter administration trade officials concerned with a steeply rising U.S. trade deficit with Japan, with a 10 percent U.S. unemployment rate, and with securing Japanese tariff reduction and market liberalization commitments at the Tokyo Round of multilateral trade negotiations under the General Agreement for Tariffs and Trade (GATT) framework. The GATT provided an institutional and legal environment for establishing, revising, and enforcing agreed-on rules for the conduct of trade among nations. GATT dispute-settlement procedures were available for both Washington and Tokyo.

In practice, the GATT often functioned as a multilateral cover for bilateral deals between trading partners. The GATT structure—a law-based, universalistic, consensus-based regime—also provided a useful forum for discussions, a place where governments could achieve some anonymity—and some delay—by multilateralizing an issue that would otherwise be dealt with bilaterally. At the same time, the GATT's system for handling trade-related disputes provided governments with a potentially powerful threat for noncompliance. The Japanese-U.S. negotiations on citrus products took place against a GATT backdrop, but the two governments, not the GATT membership or institutional structure, would decide how the issue would be resolved.

Over the next eleven years, the United States and Japan continued to wrangle over opening the Japanese market to U.S. oranges. Although the effort was not fruitless, the process by which that success was achieved did nothing to build bilateral trust and goodwill.

Our analysis of the first negotiation, leading to the agreement signed in 1978, depicts a three-stage bargaining process: early phase, middle phase, and endgame. To avoid repetition, only a more general narrative of the latter two negotiations, leading to the agreements signed in 1983 and 1988, is presented here.[1]

ROUND ONE: NEGOTIATING THE 1978 AGREEMENT

Early Phase

In the fall of 1977, American representatives presented three general requests to Japanese Foreign Ministry officials, asking Japan to participate in reviving the international economy, to correct the bilateral U.S.-Japan trade imbalance, and to import more American agricultural products. Tokyo responded positively to the first two items, but flatly rejected the third. The

Japanese official answer, along with a specific statement that no promises were implied, contained a pledge "to study" *(kento suru)* the matter.[2]

In October 1977, the U.S. side detailed its requests in a proposal to which it sought an immediate Japanese reply. At the same time, several high-ranking officials in the office of the U.S. Special Trade Representative (STR) sharply criticized the Japanese: one official faulted Tokyo for "victimizing" Japanese consumers with overpriced farm products, while another issued a thinly veiled threat of American retaliation if Japan failed to respond by a U.S.-set deadline of mid-December. None of this American pressure moved Takeo Fukuda's government to act. At this preliminary stage of discussions, the Japanese leadership lacked the required "sense of crisis" *(kikikan)* to react promptly to Washington's package.[3] The agriculture minister, Zenko Suzuki, expressed his ministry's stance as one of "absolute opposition" *(zettai hantai)*.[4]

Rhetoric aside, however, the Japanese side's bargaining position was weak. To begin with, other agricultural sectors had been liberalized in the past, and the Japanese archipelago had not sunk beneath the sea. In addition, imports of oranges and orange products in 1976 amounted to less than 7 percent of Japan's total farm imports. Washington calculated that shipping more oranges to the Japanese would mean an extra $15 to $20 million, a hefty sum for U.S. producers, perhaps, but a miniscule half of one percent of the nearly $4 billion American trade deficit with Japan in 1976. Still another source of weakness was basic disagreement within the Japanese government on the question: the Foreign Ministry was willing—to its critics, even eager—to sacrifice the interests of another ministry, the Ministry of Agriculture, Forestry, and Fisheries, on the altar of appeasing the United States on a featherweight topic to avert possible American retaliation against Japan's heavyweight economic sectors.

Interestingly, opinions were mixed inside the Agriculture Ministry itself, and the newly appointed chief of the bureau handling Japanese producers' interests was far less ardently opposed to higher orange imports than his hard-line predecessor had been.[5] Further, Agriculture's ability to protect or advance its interests in turf battles with other ministries was diminishing. Several factors contributed to the ministry's relative decline in the Japanese bureaucracy. For one thing, the workload on Agriculture Ministry officials was daunting, even in a nation of workaholics. Too few officials (some thirty in the International Section of the ministry's Economic Bureau) with responsibility for trade-related problems had to handle a large and increasing number of bilateral and multilateral agenda items, from sugar with the Australians, to salmon with the Soviets, to humpback whales at the International Whaling Commission, to Official Development Assistance food aid percentages at the Organization for Economic Cooperation and Development, to coastal states' fishing rights at the United Nations Convention on the Law of the Sea, to orange-import levels with the Americans. Another element was the shrinking importance of the rural sector in the Japanese economy, a process that inevitably diminished the relevance and political clout of rural interests in the government. Yet another Agriculture Ministry handicap stemmed from its vulnerability to agricultural interest groups and powerful Diet members from farm-dominated electoral districts.

These basic elements—the influence of powerful politicians and client groups, an ever-expanding list of issues to address, and the dispiriting reality of the inevitable decline of the agricultural sector as a force in Japan's political economy—combined to dilute the Agriculture Ministry's once-vaunted clout. Moreover, no matter how seasoned and savvy Agriculture bureaucrats were in the nuts-and-bolts intricacies of localized agricultural politics, they lacked the linguistic, public relations, overall policymaking, and international negotiating experience of Foreign Ministry and Ministry of International Trade and Industry (MITI) officials.

Finally, as a rising economic power with a sizable and swelling current account surplus, Japan was starting in the mid-1970s to draw flak for not playing a role commensurate with its economic stature.

Uppermost in Fukuda's mind as the negotiating process began may have been American unhappiness with bilateral economic affairs, notably the trade imbalance between the United States and Japan. Responding positively to the American desire to access the Japanese domestic market for oranges would not, of course, accomplish much toward resolving the trade imbalance or broader problems. However, by demonstrating his government's readiness to deal with items on the proposed U.S. agenda—even the relatively economically inconsequential matter of orange imports—Fukuda hoped not only to ease existing trade tensions but also to help avoid future friction with Japan's dominant trading partner.

Fukuda Picks His Negotiating Team

Shortly after the first American proposals were presented, Fukuda decided to reshuffle his cabinet. Party politics was the main reason for the decision, no doubt, but trade-related negotiations with the United States may also have been a factor. The new lineup altered the domestic balance of political forces, which, in turn, shaped the way in which Tokyo would answer U.S. demands on orange imports. A shift in the political balance would also influence Fukuda's chances of securing a domestic bureaucratic and political consensus supporting his policies toward trade with the United States. Without such a consensus, Fukuda would be sure to fail in his ambitions.

The importance of establishing an internal consensus on negotiating positions has been emphasized by some of Japan's most seasoned negotiators. One of these, the veteran diplomat Tatsuo Takeda, has written that the Japanese government cannot expect to undertake negotiations effectively until and unless those in charge of the negotiations are able—by being attentive to "domestic adjustment"—to "achieve unity" *(ipponka)* among, and even within, the ministries and agencies of the Japanese government.[6] Makoto Utsumi, who was a senior Finance Ministry official in Japanese delegations for the Structural Impediments Initiative (SII) talks and for many summits of the G7 group of large industrial countries, states the point more bluntly than Takeda. "To negotiate effectively," Utsumi asserts, "Japan must have someone in Tokyo with the clout to force resolution of an issue when ministries and agencies see a situation from their own perspectives."[7]

In the Japanese government, as in Japanese society as a whole, harmony is prized and hierarchy respected. However, while Japan is a vertically organized society, it is also structured horizontally, and at each level there are numerous groups (almost independent domains) fiercely assertive of their interests and locked into competition with one another. To reduce the level of disruptive conflict among these groups, the Japanese seek to combine them in a mutually accommodative way; thus, decisions are not so much reached as arranged, with each of the different domains being recognized as having legitimacy in the decision-making process. An effective Japanese leader is one who can devise a way of either accommodating the interests of each group or compensating those groups whose interests are harmed by an agreement. Unlike countries in which the executive enjoys considerable freedom of action in the conduct of foreign policy, Japan always negotiates on at least two fronts: with another country at the negotiating table and with itself in a seamless web of consensus building. The latter begins in bureaucratic offices by day but then continues in less formal and therefore in Japanese eyes more productive consultations after hours, somewhere in the labyrinth of members-only corners of such exclusive Tokyo districts as Akasaka or the Ginza. Come morning, perhaps, a negotiating deal has been arranged, possibly at a price less exacting than that of the previous evening's entertainment.

When it came time select his cabinet, Fukuda chose people he knew and trusted—individuals whose political outlook resembled his own. Over the course of negotiations during the next year, he would permit them considerable authority over negotiating a revised pact with the United States on citrus fruit. However, he undoubtedly selected people for cabinet posts less because of their ability to deal with Americans and other foreigners than because of their skills at developing a unified position among institutions, politicians, and other influential figures at home.

For the cabinet-level position of special economic adviser, Fukuda named Nobuhiko Ushiba, who had long experience in American affairs, including a much-praised stint as ambassador to the United States in the early 1970s. Not coincidentally, Ushiba's ambassadorial tenure had coincided with Fukuda's service as foreign minister. Along with his expertise and past links to the prime minister, the pro-American Ushiba had another, potentially invaluable, asset for handling the upcoming negotiations with the United States: as a career bureaucrat with experience as bureau chief of key economic affairs bureaus in both MITI and the Foreign Ministry, he knew how to orchestrate consensus among bureaucratic fiefdoms. Politically quite conservative, Ushiba could deal effectively with Liberal Democratic Party (LDP) politicians—nearly half of whom backed farmers' interests.

Most important to negotiations on agricultural products was the minister of agriculture. For this pivotal slot, Fukuda named the youngish, action-oriented Ichiro Nakagawa. Representing a rural Hokkaido district, and savvy about farm subjects, the new minister had served as parliamentary vice minister, a key party-filled slot, in the Finance Ministry when Fukuda headed that ministry. As a leader of the right-wing Seirankai Diet members' group, Nakagawa's conservative credentials were impeccable. Nakagawa replaced the incumbent Suzuki, a die-hard defender of domestic farmers' interests, who, some conjectured, might have resigned from the agriculture post rather than submit to raised levels of foreign farm products. Nakagawa was prepared to try his hand at arranging a workable domestic consensus on upping import quotas for oranges and other related agricultural items mentioned in the American draft proposal. Indeed, as developments over the following year would show, Fukuda's government would confront far thornier problems in dealing with domestic political adversaries than in dealing with the Americans at the conference table. Nakagawa's appointment and his performance were thus of critical significance.

The new agricultural minister hit the ground running. Nakagawa's position on the issue of orange imports—a position he shared with Ushiba, other top cabinet leaders, and Fukuda himself—was that liberalization-based formulas were out of bounds. A quota-based formula, and higher quotas established on that basis, however, was quite another—and entirely negotiable—matter. As long as complete liberalization of the market for oranges was barred from the negotiating agenda, Japan's policymakers were confident they could convince the domestic political and bureaucratic adversaries to accept higher levels of quota-based orange imports.

In his public statements, Nakagawa sought refuge in ambiguity. While espousing the "absolute opposition" line palatable to domestic protectionists, he scattered hints that compromises were in the works. An example is this push-me-pull-you comment: "We cannot simply agree to liberalize oranges and other products; but I want to try in some better way. I'll study the matter at once."[8]

For his part, Ushiba, before traveling to Washington to "assess the situation" (*jokyo handan*—an essential element of the *nemawashi* process of building consensus, particularly during preliminary and early-stage bargaining), undertook the politically critical preliminary consultations with appropriate officials from the Ministry of Agriculture and MITI. MITI bureaucrats wanted the Japanese side to offer nothing until and unless the Americans asked for something specific. Ministry of Agriculture officials wanted higher import quotas to be applied to manufactured goods (but of course in MITI's domain!) rather than farm products.

Fearing that official hints and activities meant the government was preparing to sacrifice their interests, the top three agricultural interest groups launched an all-out defensive campaign under the "absolute opposition" banner, organizing demonstrations, issuing statements, and sending letters of appeal to government officials, ministry bureaucrats, and those LDP politicians sitting on party agricultural committees. The Liberal Democrats were the most receptive to these pleas, and both of the party's most powerful councils on farm-related matters—the Agricultural Committee and the Agricultural Affairs Investigative Council—passed resolutions backing the farm lobby's "absolute opposition" to increased citrus imports.[9]

This flurry of activity preceded Ushiba's submission in December of the Japanese side's opening position, a six-point reply to Washington's proposals made two months earlier. The counterproposal set forth Tokyo's starting offers on various items, from zero tariffs on autos, to modest imports of beef for hotel use, to higher import quotas for oranges and fruit juice.

On the pivotal issue of orange-import quotas, Ushiba offered a 22,500-ton increase, from 15,000 to 37,500 tons a year. This offer, which the Japanese side fully expected would be unacceptable to the Americans,[10] was the maximum level that domestic political interests in Japan were willing to tolerate at that stage. The Japanese side's game plan was to submit the offer and then use the anticipated U.S. rejection to persuade domestic opponents to accede to a higher offer.[11] Such *gaiatsu* is the straw that stirs the drink in Japanese-American negotiations. Typically sensationalized in the Japanese press, *gaiatsu* is used, and not infrequently even solicited, by reformist Japanese in need of some extra muscle in convincing die-hard intransigents to accept an otherwise unacceptable agenda item.

Washington performed the role it was supposed to play in this scenario. As expected, Japan's package fell short of American expectations. After turning down the Japanese proposal as wholly inadequate, Special Trade Representative Robert Strauss scrubbed plans to go to Tokyo to finish the agreement, pending a more forthcoming Japanese response.

As the U.S. side was assailing the Japanese government for offering too little, domestic interests in Japan were pummeling the government for offering too much. Of the six points in the Japanese response, farmers' groups were most distressed with a single item, the one dealing with citrus products and beef. Farmers' nightmares of a government sellout of their interests seemed to be coming true.

Farm lobby activists, doubtful that the Fukuda government (and the Foreign Ministry especially) would be much inclined to favor their point of view in the negotiations, decided to act on their own. The main agricultural-interest organizations swiftly assembled and dispatched their own delegation to Washington for meetings with U.S agricultural groups, Carter administration trade officials, and members of Congress. Their goal was to explain the situation facing the Japanese agricultural sector. Liberal Democratic Party agricultural affairs leaders reacted in identical fashion, sponsoring their own mission to the United States.

"Mission Impossible" might be used to describe this LDP-sponsored delegation's quest for American understanding of Japan's position. However, the ostensible rationale for dispatching such a delegation was not in fact the real rationale.

Five Japanese delegations (three LDP, one Komeito, one Agricultural Cooperatives) visited the United States during the course of negotiating this first orange-import agreement. Such Japanese-sponsored missions have become an established element in the ritualized stagecraft of Japanese-American diplomacy. On the surface, these delegations have served two goals. First, they have been fact-finders, seeking information about U.S. policies and positions through personal meetings with various American experts, officials, and politicians. Second, they have been surrogates for the government, attempting to explain Japan's position, to appeal to Americans for understanding, to describe Japan's great efforts at resolving a problem, and to communicate such things as Japanese sincerity, resolve, unity, and true intentions. Few Japanese missions have ferreted out any facts not already known to the officials who sent them, and fewer still have changed Americans' minds with rhetoric and passion.

However quixotic they might appear to Americans, these Japanese delegations play a major—even essential—role in the later scenes of the bilateral bargaining drama. Delegation members acquire legitimacy and credibility as having been players in the process. Their nationalistic bona fides are confirmed by their having pleaded Japan's case, however unsuccessfully, to influential Americans. Typically, later on in negotiations, when the Japanese side must face and force the issue of compromise, delegation members emerge from the wings to play the role of facilitators for flexibility, confirming government negotiators' judgments that Japanese concessions must be offered to "save the situation." In short, such delegations perform in America to an attentive—and influential—Japanese audience.

Thus, it is not surprising that neither of the two orange-related Japanese delegations accomplished what each had hoped officially to achieve. One STR official, for instance, dismissed the farm group's arguments as "irrational."[12] As for bending the U.S. side toward appreciating the Japanese viewpoint, the double-barreled strategy clearly failed. In the case of the party-sponsored mission, in fact, the effort seems to have backfired. Exposure to the firmness of the American position and U.S. domestic political and economic conditions (for instance, the upcoming congressional elections, double-digit unemployment, and rising protectionism) made the delegation's party leaders shift their thinking by 180 degrees.[13]

These nongovernmental efforts, however, at least seemed to reinforce the belief in Tokyo that "we must make clear what we are prepared to and not prepared to compromise about."[14] The two nongovernmental missions, in short, helped persuade domestic hard-liners to accept as inevitable the higher levels of imported oranges the United States was demanding.

Given the expected American dismissal of Tokyo's initial offer and the unexpected volte face in the LDP-sponsored delegation's stance, Fukuda was now equipped to make a decision. He concluded that only if the Japanese side agreed to triple the existing quota, to 45,000 tons a year, could it expect to reach a settlement. Fukuda turned to his minister of agriculture to prepare the groundwork with party politicians and ministry officials. Nakagawa had little difficulty carrying out his assignment: the party's American mission had made farm policy politicians more flexible, and officials willing to follow Nakagawa's leadership had been appointed to key Agriculture Ministry positions. Nakagawa thought the inevitable domestic backlash against the 45,000-ton figure would subside once an agreement was reached with the Americans.[15]

Farm lobby predictions that "even if you can't see them yet, the Black Ships are coming!" and Japanese news accounts that Fukuda had decided to up imports dramatically were confirmed a month later when the two governments announced an agreement that included tripling the annual import quota for oranges from 15,000 to 45,000 tons.

Middle Phase

The January agreement proved illusory, however. In May 1978, the American side, contrary to Tokyo's expectations, placed on the negotiating table new items that extended beyond the domestic consensus Nakagawa had so carefully pieced together in late 1977. Now Washington wanted a wider, four-month seasonal window (May through August instead of June through August) for imported oranges, and access by new firms to the expanded market for imported oranges. These new demands reflected effective political arm-twisting by Senator Richard Stone of Florida on behalf of his state's orange growers.[16]

Soon after this, following the release of figures for 1977 that showed a record trade deficit with Japan, the U.S. side yet again moved the negotiating goalposts. Not only was Washington continuing to press for the expanded seasonal window, it was also now asking for import quotas far higher than the 45,000-ton amount agreed to in January. But the most significant, and to the Japanese side most puzzling, part of the new proposal was the American demand that both wider seasonal and overall access (via yearly incremental hikes) to the Japanese domestic orange market be based on the principle of liberalization (*jiyuka*).

The Japanese responded, as they had the previous fall, by ruling out of bounds any agreement based on liberalization. Moreover, Tokyo officially refused to negotiate on the basis of the latest U.S. proposals because, in its view, the total amounts and the rate of annual increases for orange imports had been settled already in the January agreement.[17]

During the spring, however, the unity of the Japanese government crumbled. Ushiba was the first to bend, probably because of pressure on him from STR Strauss and Ambassador Mansfield, and because of his worries, appropriate to the nature of his cabinet portfolio, about the approaching deadline for conclusion of the Tokyo Round of trade deliberations. No doubt Ushiba realized that in previous negotiating engagements with the Americans, and despite prolonged resistance, haggling, delay, and confrontation, the Japanese side eventually had succumbed, again and again, to the bulk of American demands. Repeatedly, too, Japanese capitulation had occurred at the final, even last-minute, stage of negotiations as Japanese political leaders had become personally engaged in the process and orchestrated Japanese concessions rather than endangering the overall relationship with the United States. Ushiba's shift toward a more accommodating line was hinted at in a statement he made on April 13, in which he dismissed the preceding U.S.-Japan negotiations on oranges as a "preliminary skirmish" and added, "The real battle is yet to come."[18]

With Ushiba's adoption of a conciliatory line—a position Fukuda supported—Nakagawa's continued defense of the January compromise level became politically untenable. Nevertheless, he remained both loyal to Fukuda and determined to execute his responsibilities as agriculture minister in resolving the issue. As was the case during the preliminary negotiating period, his most challenging task was winning over the Liberal Democrat politicians in control of the agriculture-related committees in the party. This was the proper target: the lobbying efforts of farm activists and orange importers (whose views varied) were aimed at these politicians. Dealing with the politicians would take care of the bureaucrats. Ministry bureaucrats did not pose a problem, as they both respected him and shared his position on the negotiations—namely, compromise on issues other than liberalization.

Once the domestic reevaluation of the Japanese position began, the previous fall's pattern of hard-line rhetoric punctuated with suggestions of compromise resurfaced in officials' statements. Leaders who publicly dismissed any possibility of reopening talks on oranges in the same breath hinted at softness in the Japanese position. For instance, Nakagawa diluted the credibility of his otherwise convincing "No" to renewed negotiations by this oblique comment: "Should the coming situation change, we may go so far as to think about studying the matter."[19] Similarly, in a July 10 press conference, Nakagawa first expressed his exasperation with the American negotiating demands ("We can't do what we can't do") and then proceeded to voice his readiness to "try" (ganbaru) his best "on the basis of compromise" to gain an agreement.[20] Translation: Tokyo now was assessing what concessions would be required if the negotiations reopened.

Whether the American negotiators' antennae picked up these subtle signals from the Japanese side is an open question. Japanese farm lobby activists, however, ever vigilant for the faintest sign of governmental waffling, certainly needed no translation. Perceiving Tokyo to be ready once again to sacrifice their interests for the sake of an accord with Washington, the main farmers' interest groups reacted as they had before. They launched yet another round of demonstrations. They circulated yet another series of emotional petitions to government officials. And they set about organizing and dispatching yet another delegation to explain the conditions facing Japan's farmers to American politicians and trade officials.

This time around, however, their zealous efforts (for example, printing a mass of pamphlets and distributing them to American officials and politicians) were too much for Tokyo officials, who accused the farm lobbyists of interfering in the negotiating process.[21]

During the summer, pressures intensified on the Japanese government to work toward a new agreement. President Carter sent a personal note to Fukuda. At July's Bonn summit, other G7 leaders would be expecting to hear the Japanese explain their position on tariffs, market liberalization, and—perhaps—even orange imports. American trade officials continued to press their Japanese counterparts on the subject. Fukuda personally wanted to wrap up negotiations before his party's presidential election in late fall. And the January 1979 deadline for concluding the Tokyo Round trade negotiations loomed ominously on the horizon.[22]

Final Phase

During the summer months, the two LDP agricultural policy kingpins, Eiichi Nakao and Takami Eto, journeyed to the United States once again. In what was a frequent ritual ceremony in these negotiations, Nakagawa himself visited Washington "to explain the real situation facing Japanese agriculture." The agriculture minister returned to Japan more determined to carry out the task of bringing new firms into the orange-import business—just as the American side had been urging.[23] In the end, the accumulation of visits, pressures, and deadlines brought Tokyo back to the negotiating table.

The American side had presented its revised package in May and had restated its position in June, in advance of the Bonn summit. After a long summer of deliberations, the Japanese side submitted its counterdraft to Strauss and the American team in September, to begin three days of negotiations in Washington. Strauss quickly rejected Japan's proposals.

The morning after receiving and spurning the Japanese counterdraft, the American team tabled its final plan. Interestingly, whereas the Japanese side had spent four grueling months preparing its September proposal, the Americans drafted and submitted their response in less than a day.

Japanese negotiators, who still clung tenaciously to the gist of the January agreement, expressed "shock" (*shokku*, the term Japanese invariably use when reacting to some dramatic turn of events—Nixon's opening to China, the Arab oil embargo, or even, in this case, the prospect of a few hundred million U.S.-grown oranges coming into Japan) at the new American plan.[24] They were irritated as well. Yet again, it seemed, the Americans had shifted their position, this time on the subject of access by new firms to the Japanese orange-import market. In addition, Japanese negotiators were irked by what they perceived as inconsistency and mixed messages in the U.S. handling of the negotiations. As Nakagawa explained it:

> What surprises me in this round of the negotiations with the United States is the American attitude. What the Americans say in Geneva is what the Americans say in Geneva, but not elsewhere. The Americans stress their unhappiness with our draft. My impression from my own earlier conversations with Ambassador Mansfield and from Ambassador Togo's talks with Mansfield is that the focus is now different than it was before.[25]

At the same time, one must recall it was the agriculture minister himself who had wanted to defer compromise on the issue of access by new firms, until the U.S. side turned up the pressure. Thus, the new U.S. stance could not have come as a complete shock to Nakagawa and the Japanese side. In fact, American *gaiatsu* provided Nakagawa, who favored the idea anyway, with exactly the weapon he wanted (and had expected to receive) and could now bring to bear on those still resisting compromise on the issue.

The negotiations stalled briefly after the September exchange of proposals, but the two sides managed to reach agreement the following month. Beginning with a 65,000-ton orange-import level for 1980, the accord provided for gradual increases through 1983 to an annual quota of 85,200 tons. For its part, the U.S. side withdrew its demand, first presented in May and repeated several times thereafter, for gradual liberalization of the market for oranges. This, however, is properly seen as a sham concession on a topic both sides recognized to be beyond the scope of the actual bargaining agenda at that stage. During this negotiating phase, the bargaining was over import-quota levels, with liberalization, by mutual agreement, remaining off the agenda.

Final agreement, instead, stemmed from Japanese concessions—on all three major bargaining issues: the amount of annual imports of oranges, the extent to which new firms would participate in the orange-import and -distribution system, and the seasonal import period (extended to four rather than three months). Three times during the yearlong negotiations, the U.S. side had changed its position on the terms it wanted. Three times over the same period the Japanese side, after recovering and adjusting to the new American positions, had acceded to them, albeit holding fast on the principle of liberalization. In the end, the Japanese government accepted a final package containing items it had rejected a year earlier and several times thereafter.

Even after the basic agreement was reached, Nakagawa made one final attempt—perfunctorily, and without success—to improve the terms but, in the end, Tokyo decided to leave well enough alone and proceed along lines previously approved at the administrative level of the three ministries involved (MITI, Agriculture, and the Foreign Ministry) and the LDP agricultural policy committees.

ROUND TWO: NEGOTIATING THE 1983 AGREEMENT

Negotiations to extend the 1978 bilateral accord, which applied only to fiscal years 1980–83, began in November 1981 and lasted through 1983, when an agreement was reached covering the four-year period 1984–87. Compared with the 1977–78 negotiations, these were relatively straightforward and can be summarized briefly.

The process of negotiating was launched in late 1981 by a set of American proposals that called for total Japanese liberalization of imports of twenty-two agricultural products and threatened an appeal to a GATT panel if Tokyo failed to comply. The ambitious nature of these requests stemmed from several developments on the U.S. side, including the desire of the new Reagan administration to open foreign markets to U.S. exports, the increasingly widespread view among Americans that Japan's domestic market was not sufficiently open to foreign products, and rising protectionist sentiments in the Congress and the executive branch.

President Reagan's offer of a basket of American oranges ("Eat up, they're not contaminated") to Prime Minister Suzuki elicits a "No, thank you."

Sankei shimbun, March 10, 1982. Cartoon by Tsuchida Naotoshi. Reproduced with permission.

The Japanese side approached the negotiations warily, even offering what might be called an anticipatory concession. Expecting U.S. criticism over the strict Japanese inspection system for imported citrus products, Tokyo revamped the process before negotiations began, in hopes of defusing a flap on the subject.[26] The gesture proved ineffective, however, for Washington's interests were far more ambitious than simplifying the inspection process. Voicing surprise at the harshness of U.S. demands, Japanese negotiators rejected the proposals. Throughout these exchanges, Japanese officials seemed perplexed by Washington's pursuit of liberalization or increased import quotas based on the principle of liberalization.[27] In Japanese eyes, the Americans should have known these demands to be totally beyond the maximum possible range of Japanese concessions.

During the negotiations, Japan's position gradually eroded, but only up to the liberalization limit. Because other products of lesser significance to the Japanese than oranges and beef were involved, Tokyo attempted to soften the American stance by making "sacrificial" concessions on these peripheral items (for example, tomato paste).[28] The ploy failed to budge Washington from its step-by-step campaign to achieve total liberalization or to win counterconcessions in other areas.

The Japanese side's official rejections, preemptive concessions, and sacrificial offerings failed to alter Washington's position on many issues. However, the Ministry of Agriculture's stubborn refusal to bend on the subject did eventually bring the U.S. side to withdraw its demand for total elimination of import restrictions; in return, the Japanese agreed to increase the import quotas for oranges by a further 44,000 tons, with the increase to come into effect gradually over the four-year term of the agreement. As in the earlier round of bargaining on orange imports, the exchanges that led to this withdrawal reflected the fundamental parry-and-thrust nature of Japanese-American interactions on market-access issues.[29]

ROUND THREE: NEGOTIATING THE 1988 AGREEMENT

When the second four-year agreement was concluded in 1983, William Brock, the United States Trade Representative (USTR, as the STR had been renamed in 1979) submitted a letter to the Japanese ambassador. The letter stated the American understanding that Japan would liberalize its market for oranges completely after 1987, the final year of the bilateral orange-import accord of 1983. The Japanese side, however, refused to accept this American interpretation of Japan's commitment.

Nonetheless, during 1987, the final year covered by the 1983 accord, U.S. officials and politicians waged an intense campaign of political pressure and hectoring to force Japan to open its domestic market to imported oranges, and also beef and rice. In January 1988, Prime Minister Noboru Takeshita met President Ronald Reagan in Washington. The two leaders agreed to pursue liberalization on these products at the bilateral level, against the backdrop of the expiring 1983 agreement. When the United States declared that if no new agreement was arranged by the end of March it would submit the issue to a GATT panel—and thus oblige Tokyo to address the larger question of liberalization within a multilateral forum— Japan decided to negotiate the issue.

From the outset of the bilateral talks, which continued for six months, Tokyo's goals were to focus the discussions as narrowly as possible; to address only a single subject, beef (not a package deal including oranges and rice as well); and to negotiate bilaterally, avoiding consideration of the subject at the multilateral GATT level. The Japanese side wanted no agreement, no commitment to a timetable for liberalization, and indeed no negotiations at all; but once it had consented to negotiate, its concern was to limit any negotiated settlement as much as possible. In particular, Japan sought to fight off liberalization of its orange-import market or, if liberalization proved irresistible, to delay it for as long as possible.

As the negotiations began, the Japanese side rejected the idea of a timetable for liberalization, but it quickly caved in on that topic. Japanese representatives sought out personal meetings with American officials to express how difficult liberalization was for Japan, to appeal for understanding of Japan's difficult situation, and to point out the unfairness of singling out Japanese quotas and import restrictions when others (e.g., the European Community on imported high-quality beef; the United States on foreign cheese and dairy products) likewise imposed barriers to protect economically uncompetitive but politically significant agricultural interests.[30]

These defensive efforts proved futile. Japan did not oppose inclusion of citrus products on the negotiating agenda, and during the early phase of the negotiations it accepted the inevitability of liberalization. However, when no further progress was made as the March deadline approached, the discussions were broken off (euphemistically described as "adjourned" by the Japanese side), with Tokyo expressing surprise at the U.S. position and Washington determined to take the issue before the GATT panel.

Japan blocked the GATT panel and pressed hard for the issue to be handled bilaterally. Thereafter, Japan sought to gain time before liberalization; to avoid making unilateral concessions and to obtain American concessions through contingent offers; to criticize the United States for making excessive demands; to continue to appeal to the U.S. side for understanding of Japan's situation; and to postpone reaching agreement on oranges.

Japan's bid for time was explained by the need for Takeshita, a relatively powerful Japanese leader, to arrange the necessary domestic consensus that would support the compromises judged necessary. Concessions on

oranges, along with beef and other agricultural products, struck at the economic heart of the LDP's core rural constituency. Farmers were represented by powerful lobbying organizations and by powerful LDP politicians at the top levels of government. Disagreement within the Japanese
side reflected deep internal cleavages on farm-related issues. Accordingly,
the most daunting political task was arranging a domestic consensus firm
enough to sustain unity among the Japanese team when compromise became unavoidable during the final phase of negotiations.

Takeshita's challenge was formidable, but he was able to orchestrate the
domestic political adjustments needed to meet the American demands.
Japanese compromises stemmed from a fear of being hauled before the
GATT; a desire to avoid embarrassment and pressure at the Toronto summit in July; concern about the "overall U.S.-Japan relationship"; and, oddly,
the perception that "if Japan did not concede, an agreement would not be
possible."[31] Throughout the negotiations, even when pursuing tactics of
issue avoidance and issue minimization (e.g., lengthy delays in responding,
ambiguously stated commitments, self-serving rationalizations, appeals for
consideration of Japan's "special" situation), the Japanese continued to participate in the process of bargaining.

Why the Japanese side persisted in bargaining hard with a weak hand
is intriguing analytically, particularly in light of the heavy Japanese stress
on situational perception as a negotiating norm. Intriguing, too, is the
extent to which the orange-imports case, arguably among the least intel-
lectually challenging items on the U.S.-Japan bilateral economic agenda,
illustrates the patterns that appear to be embedded in Japanese negotiating behavior. Had the Japanese side bent easily and quickly on liberal-
izing Japan's orange market to foreign-grown imports, Japan might have
improved its stature as a cooperative trading partner, avoided a considerable amount of criticism, and benefited by focusing its bureaucratic and
political resources on more significant topics. Instead, the Japanese chose
to react and resist, thus missing whatever gains might have accrued to
Japan by yielding with good grace. It appears that the Japanese manner of
negotiating is so deeply ingrained as to be beyond conscious adjustment
to circumstances. As will be seen in the following chapters, Japanese representatives seem to have acted similarly when negotiating on oranges and
when bargaining over fighter planes or rice imports. This consistency of

approach suggests that Japanese bargaining behavior does not vary significantly according to the subject being negotiated.

The agreement finally reached in mid-June 1988 was a solid victory for the United States, the aggressive side throughout the process. Consistently on the defensive, the Japanese side's successes were modest and were scored in low-risk engagements at the negotiating perimeter, when Japan was able to concede a bit less than Washington asked. On yearly orange-import amounts, Japan gradually raised its offers. Japan's preferred five-year delay before liberalization was squeezed gradually to three years for oranges and four years for orange juice.

CONCLUSION

How should we judge the effectiveness of Japanese negotiating behavior in the case of bargaining with the United States over orange imports? In 1977 Japan avowed its determination not to liberalize its market; fourteen years later, Japan phased out its quota-based controls. Thus we have a clear picture of a Japanese defeat. Or do we? Certainly, Japan retreated in the face of U.S. pressure during each round of negotiations, but on each occasion it was a measured retreat, not an unconditional surrender. Moreover, if one assumes (as the Japanese may have done from quite early on) that eventual liberalization of orange imports was inevitable under the GATT rules, delaying the inevitable by fourteen years could even be seen as a kind of victory.

The first accord, signed in December 1978, provided for an initial raising of the import quota for oranges from 15,000 to 65,000 tons a year, followed by a further gradual increase over the fiscal 1980–83 period to 85,200 tons. Japanese trade negotiators thus agreed to substantial increases in orange imports, but they successfully resisted American urging to liberalize the orange market by removing quantitative restrictions altogether.

The second agreement, concluded in April 1984 after over a year and a half of intensive discussions, likewise reflected a compromise: significantly higher levels of orange imports by Japan, but still no liberalization. This agreement also covered a four-year period, with Japan promising an increase in the orange quota of 44,000 metric tons, spread over the period of the agreement.

In the third and last orange-related accord, signed in June 1988, Japan finally agreed to phase out quota-based controls over orange imports. Foreign orange purchases were to increase by 22,000 metric tons annually, or a total of 66,000 metric tons over the three years 1988–90; on April 1, 1991, import quotas on oranges were to be abolished altogether.

Japan's overall negotiating posture can best be described as reactive and defensive. On no occasion did it initiate negotiations, and on each occasion it sought to minimize the scope of the issues on the bargaining table. Its negotiators moved slowly, partly in an effort to wear down the U.S. side, partly because of the need to establish a consensus within Japanese political and bureaucratic circles before adopting or adapting a negotiating position. Typically, at the start of a new round of negotiations, prominent Japanese political figures would express shock at the extent of American demands and publicly declare their steadfast opposition to any compromise—again, a tactic aimed both at the U.S. side and at domestic opinion—but then, as U.S. pressure mounted, they would begin to signal, obliquely at first, a readiness to contemplate accommodating U.S. interests. Finally, Japanese leaders would use *gaiatsu* for their own purposes, as a stick with which to beat die-hard opponents into line.

Such a defensive, reactive, and ultimately accommodating posture may seem less than heroic—certainly it seemed that way to many Japanese interest groups and journalists. However, given not only Japan's awareness of its subordinate position in its relationship with the United States but also the Japanese tendency to seek out harmony and consensus at home while avoiding criticism and isolation abroad, a defensive approach to negotiations is entirely understandable. As the following two chapters show, it is an approach that has characterized other Japanese negotiating encounters with the United States since the end of World War II.

2

NEGOTIATIONS ON RICE IMPORTS, 1986–93

Michael Blaker

For Japan, rice is a near-sacred product, deeply embedded in Japanese history, culture, economics, politics, and symbolism. The Japanese ideograph for *I* is a combination of the character for a sheaf of rice and the character meaning nose. One's self, in short, is tied to one's rice. During the Tokugawa Era (1615–1868), rice was the Japanese economic medium of exchange, with the standard measurement being a *koku*—the amount of rice one person would consume during one year. Whereas (as we saw in the previous chapter) the Japanese were reluctant to open their orange market to foreign imports, they were adamant that the doors to their rice market would remain tightly closed. "Not a single grain of foreign rice shall ever enter Japan" was the solemn vow of Japanese politicians of all stripes, backed by public opinion, the press, the business community, academics, and the bureaucracy. In reality, Japan had imported considerable rice from Korea and Taiwan before 1945. This fact, however, was largely ignored, and opposition to the import of rice reflected a national consensus.

Small wonder, then, that when the United States demanded in 1986 that Japan open its rice market, Japanese history and culture were used as an argument for protectionism. Over seven years would pass, and six prime ministers would hold office, before a negotiated settlement was reached in December 1993. In the intervening years, as negotiations alternated between a bilateral and a multilateral forum, Japan would employ a wide array of techniques first to try to avoid discussing the subject at all and then to try to minimize the scope of discussions and the content of subsequent compromises. Yet, while Japan was active and—for a long time—adamant in its opposition to the U.S. demands for

market access, it was undoubtedly on the defensive throughout the negotiating process. As with the negotiations on orange imports, these negotiations demonstrated many elements of the "coping" approach that perme-
ates Japanese diplomatic activity (see the introductory chapter, p. 6). In
particular, the negotiations highlighted the fundamentally reactive, cautious, defensive, and slow-paced nature of Japanese diplomacy.

The negotiations over rice also exposed how powerfully domestic
institutions and processes shape Japanese diplomacy, notably the importance of building a domestic consensus to support a negotiating position
or a negotiated settlement.

As we will see, Japanese negotiators sought, to the greatest extent possible, to avoid losses and to limit damage, making incremental changes to
their negotiating position only when a domestic consensus had been
reached and only when prodded to do so by the U.S. side. Their bargaining behavior fits one American observer's apt likening of Japan's diplomatic style to that of "an interested bridge partner, waiting to follow the
first good bid from the American side."[1]

PRENEGOTIATING PHASE: NO, NO, A THOUSAND TIMES, NO!

U.S. pressure on Japan to open its rice market to foreign rice began with
the U.S. complaint in 1986 that Japanese restrictions on imports of twelve
agricultural products, including rice, were in violation of the General
Agreement on Trade and Tariffs (GATT) rules. The U.S. complaint
stemmed from prodding by a well-organized American lobbying group,
the Rice Millers' Association.

On an opposition-to-liberalization scale of one to ten, with oranges rating a three, rice would have registered a perfect ten. However, Japan was
opposed not only to liberalization—that is, removing all restrictions on
rice imports—but to importing rice even subject to restrictions, such as
quotas. The Japanese goal was simple: keep foreign rice from Japanese
mouths. Along with the heavy cultural value the Japanese attached to the
subject of rice was the virtually universal Japanese perception of the
domestic rice market as sacrosanct. Permitting foreign rice to enter Japan
was tantamount to letting foreign firms build condos inside the walls of
the Imperial Palace. The Japanese response to American demands for

opening the domestic market was akin to "How dare you!" Thus, during the prenegotiations on rice, Japan's basic objective was negative, to block the subject from being placed on the bargaining agenda at all, at either the bilateral or the multilateral GATT level.

The Rice Millers' petition was filed under section 301 of the Trade Act of 1974, which required the president to retaliate against a country deemed protectionist by Congress, with the Trade Representative's office having forty-five days to determine whether or not to accept the petition. As United States Trade Representative (USTR) Clayton Yeutter wrestled with the issue, he was the target of a Japanese defensive counterattack unleashed with every weapon available. Both houses of the Diet voted unanimously in favor of a resolution binding Japan to self-sufficiency in rice production. Politicians, the press, big business, academic experts, and of course farm lobby groups voiced a single message: "No" on rice imports. In order to communicate this resolve to the Americans—to make Washington "understand" the Japanese situation and to persuade it not to press rice importation on Japan—letters were sent, envoys were dispatched, meetings were arranged, and demonstrations were organized. The Japanese side seemed to be reading from the script used a decade earlier, during the prebargaining phase of the negotiations with the United States over textiles. At that time Tokyo launched personal appeals to American officials; the Diet unanimously passed a resolution rejecting the negotiation of import controls on textiles; and arguments were made—as they soon would be in the fight against rice imports—that the issue should be resolved through multilateral GATT procedures, not through bilateral Japanese-U.S. negotiations.[2]

Among the long list of reasons cited in support of the Japanese position in various prebargaining communications (letters, personal visits, speeches, press releases) to USTR Yeutter, key members of the Congress and Senate, the White House, business groups, and the media were the following:

❖ rice has great historical and cultural significance in Japan;

❖ other countries also award preferential treatment to certain economic sectors;

❖ Japan is already the world's leading importer of foreign agricultural products;

❖ Japan's National Food Control Law establishes rice as a "basic food" and self-sufficiency in rice as essential to national security interests;

❖ the Japanese Diet and public will never accept rice importation;

❖ Japan's situation on rice is "unique," "special," and "different";

❖ if Japan is forced to import rice, Japanese-American relations will suffer;

❖ rice is a domestic issue of no concern to other countries; and

❖ Japan needs more time to consider the subject, so other governments should be patient.[3]

EARLY PHASE: JAPAN AGREES TO NEGOTIATE ON RICE

None of these arrows drawn from the Japanese quiver of arguments found its target. USTR Yeutter's denial of the Rice Millers' petition merely brought a pause in the accelerating American campaign to pry open Japan's domestic market to U.S. rice.

Leading the American assault were U.S. politicians from rice-producing states. Early in 1987, for example, Governor George Deukmejian of California headed a state trade-promotion mission to Japan. The governor strongly urged not just imports but complete liberalization of rice in a session with Prime Minister Yasuhiro Nakasone. Deukmejian's aide stated, "If you want to get the attention of the Japanese, all you have to do is hit them over the head with a 2x4." This statement was picked up by the major American newspapers, including the *Los Angeles Times*.[4] (On a personal note, the Japanese consul general in Los Angeles asked me if I had seen the *LA Times* article. I said I had. After a long pause, he asked, "By the way, what's a '2x4'?")

In 1988, with a second Rice Millers' petition under consideration at the USTR's office, Ambassador Nobuo Matsunaga met Yeutter. After urging Yeutter to reject the petition, Matsunaga communicated Japan's willingness to include rice on the negotiating agenda of the Uruguay Round of the GATT (where, it seems, Japan expected the talks to go nowhere). Based on the ambassador's assurance, Yeutter announced his decision rejecting the Rice Millers' petition on the condition that Japan deliver on its stated commitment to address the issue multilaterally.[5]

Prime Minister Takeshita and Agriculture Minister Sato find Mike Tyson at Japan's door in a Trade Sanctions Act T-shirt delivering "beef on rice," with oranges on the side.

Yomiuri shimbun, March 17, 1988. Cartoon by Yutenji Saburo. Reproduced with permission.

As Yeutter was putting the Japanese commitment on public record, multilateral pressures on Japan were beginning to build. At the Uruguay Round in October 1988, the Cairns Group—an influential caucus of fourteen agricultural exporting nations that met first in Cairns, Australia, in August 1986—asked for "minimum access" to the Japanese rice market.[6] Japan sent a mammoth delegation to the Uruguay Round negotiations in Montreal in December, including a large *oendan*, or "supporters' group," of party politicians attending, as is typical of Japanese multilateral delegations, to gain information, to score political points by having been at the scene, to demonstrate commitment to the Japanese cause in the negotiations, and, perhaps, to keep a watchful eye on Japanese bureaucrats in case they might be inclined to compromise excessively. By the Montreal meetings, two factors combined to push Tokyo into bargaining on rice imports: Japanese official acceptance of the principle of liberalization for some agricultural products, and the risk of USTR approval of another Rice Millers' petition if Japan continued to stonewall on lifting its rice-import ban. Japan had crossed the line and was enmeshed in the negotiating process. There would be no turning back.

However, although the Japanese were now contemplating the liberalization of some of their markets for agricultural products, they were still adamant that rice not be among them. This determination had been stiffened earlier in 1988, when, during the U.S.-Japan negotiations over renewal of the agreement on imports of beef and citrus fruit, Yeutter had told the Japanese minister of agriculture, Takashi Sato, that the United States would not press Japan bilaterally to liberalize its rice market.

Also important, in Japanese eyes, was Agriculture Secretary Richard E. Lyng's statement later that year that the United States would be willing to accept a percentage-based "partial access" (in Japanese, *bubun kaiho*) arrangement for Japanese rice imports.[7] Through the summer of 1990 the Japanese were content to allow the explosive political issue of rice to remain on the multilateral shelf, as Tokyo watched and waited for circumstances that might require a Japanese response. The heated Japanese domestic political debate over the rice question was based on the premise that the Americans would allow the issue to be addressed at the GATT on the basis of "partial access"—a gradual opening of Japan's rice market—without tariffication. (Tariffication is a process by which quantitative restrictions on imports are first converted to tariff-rate equivalents— duties—which are then reduced over time to a zero level. In effect, tariffication means liberalization.)

Not surprisingly, in light of this belief that the Americans eventually would soften their "no-exceptions" opposition to special treatment for any nation's domestic agricultural sector, Japanese officials were jolted in mid-1990 when Deputy Secretary of State Lawrence R. Eagleburger informed the Japanese that partial access would not satisfy Washington. Instead, said Eagleburger, tariffication of rice imports would be required.[8]

Overnight, the rug had been yanked from under Japanese assumptions as to what type of Japanese compromise on rice would satisfy the Americans. Throughout the rice negotiations, but especially after this shift in American expectations of Japan, the Japanese side's negotiating plans and behavior turned almost exclusively on shifts in the character and nuance of positions taken by the U.S. side.[9]

One element in Japan's defensive bargaining strategy was active involvement in negotiations at the multilateral level. Tokyo's multilateralization of the rice-import question no doubt stemmed from a conviction that action could be thereby avoided, given the GATT's impoverished record in reining in protection-minded governments. As they conducted a holding pattern at the Uruguay Round, Japanese officials concentrated on the real target, the U.S. government. Consistently, the Japanese goal was to ferret out by whatever means were at their disposal what the Americans meant by their proposals, what they expected, and what minimum level of Japanese concessions they would accept.

The Japanese were quite right to focus their efforts on the Americans, for, as we will see, although the Uruguay Round provided a structural umbrella for negotiations on rice, final resolution of the rice issue was achieved via negotiations between the two governments. Japanese diplomacy buffs refer to such bilateral-in-a-multilateral-framework interactions as *maruchi-bi*. In the rice case, the critical process was to be *bi*, with not much *maruchi* impact until an impending global trade accord provided isolation-conscious Japanese leaders with a final-hour incentive to accept the previously arranged U.S.-Japan compromise formula.

MIDDLE PHASE: TO THE BRINK OF COMPROMISE AND BACK

When Kiichi Miyazawa became prime minister in November 1991, he quickly assigned top priority to working toward a successful conclusion of the Uruguay Round. His personal commitment to that process, however, did not imply that he supported a tariffication formula for rice imports. The most likely explanation was the need to cement support among Japanese voters from agricultural districts in the wake of his Liberal Democratic Party's loss of its majority in the upper house of the Diet in midyear elections. Tariffication of rice imports would mean revising the Food Control

Law. Upper house approval would be required for revising the law. Thus, as the prime minister told Secretary of State James Baker in Tokyo in November 1991, "It's impossible to accept tariffication-based rice imports, because that would require revising the Food Control Law."[10]

Japan's negotiating stance was therefore focused on locating areas of possible Japanese compromise—without changing the Food Control Law. Arthur Dunkel, the Swiss GATT secretary general, was expected to release a draft proposal on December 20. Miyazawa, anticipating the release of the Dunkel Paper, sent a former ambassador to the United States, Nobuo Matsunaga, to sound out the American side. Matsunaga met several people, including Brent Scowcroft, who expressed firmly to the envoy the American hard-line position on tariffication.[11]

As it happened, the Dunkel Paper—which was to be the basic negotiating text for the Uruguay Round agreement—did not gain enough support to succeed in Geneva. But the presentation of the 450-page Dunkel take-it-or-leave-it proposal—which ruled out special treatment for any nation's agricultural sector—forced the Japanese government to move beyond its earlier endorsement of the principle of allowing rice imports to the thornier task of implementing those lofty declarations with specific commitments. By requiring Tokyo to address the issue seriously, Dunkel's document symbolized the beginning of the middle phase of bargaining on the subject.

The Dunkel proposal also hardened the American side's no-exceptions position and shaped the approach it would adopt in discussions during 1992. U.S. officials began what would later become a chorus of criticism aimed at Japanese "intransigence," which, the Americans claimed, threatened to derail the Uruguay Round process.

Japan's response in early 1992 to the Dunkel draft raised the hackles of American negotiators, as the Japanese document excluded rice tariffication entirely. In light of the hostile U.S. reaction to the Japanese position, Miyazawa directed officials of Gaimusho (the Ministry of Foreign Affairs) and the Agriculture Ministry to work out a policy plan that would be acceptable to the United States and would not require changing the Food Control Law. Operating under these two general guidelines, Foreign Ministry bureaucrats prepared several drafts before producing a final version, which they submitted to Miyazawa in September. The Gaimusho draft set a tariff rate of between 900 and 1,000 percent—a rate that would effectively bar any foreign rice from entering Japan![12] Agriculture Ministry officials defiantly planted their feet against any compromise, even along the lines of the Gaimusho draft. One impassioned Agriculture bureaucrat invoked the fighting spirit of the samurai who had defended Edo and the Meiji emperor against an all-out attack by rebel clans over a century before: "We are the white tiger battalion. We'll fight to the death. It's the only way we can survive."[13]

A frustrated Miyazawa then summoned Hisashi Owada and Yoshiharu Hamaguchi, the top-ranking career officials in the Foreign and Agriculture Ministries, respectively, "to talk" about the rice problem. Owada was willing to discuss the topic during the meeting, but Hamaguchi was not, because, as he reportedly claimed, "management of the Food Control Law is our baby."[14]

THE AGRICULTURE MINISTRY SOFTENS ITS STANCE

The Ministry of Agriculture's intransigence softened in July 1992 with the appointment of Akio Kyotani as administrative vice minister, or *jimu-jikan*, the top bureaucratic position. Four years before, Kyotani, then chief of the Livestock Production Bureau, had participated in negotiations with the United States over beef imports. He favored opening the Japanese rice market to imports. A highly influential official, Kyotani was revered by his bureaucratic brethren in the ministry for a particular gift—a personal quality much prized in Japanese officialdom, "the ability to respond to the situation correctly" (*jokyo ni tekikaku ni taio dekiru*).[15]

In the fall of 1992, Kyotani warned members of the Liberal Democratic Party's agriculture caucusing group that negotiations with the United States would "go nowhere" unless Japan was prepared to "set forth specific numbers." According to a later newspaper account of the meeting, Kyotani asked the politicians: "Give me the responsibility to handle this."[16] Reading between the lines, we may surmise that the Japanese side, and even Agriculture Ministry officials, were now willing to use the *t* word (*tariffication*) as well as the dreaded *r* word (*rice*) in policy planning for the negotiations. From the Ministry of Agriculture's perspective, the shift was extraordinary. After all, until just a few years before, no official interested in long-term employment at the ministry would have dared utter the *r* word, much less discuss the idea of tariffication. Japan's one-dimensional "we-won't-accept-tariffication" approach had now changed profoundly.

Three influential members of the LDP agriculture-issue group were working behind the scenes to orchestrate a way for Miyazawa to reach a politically acceptable decision on rice imports. This trio of conservative politicians—Taichiro Okawara, Koichi Kato, and Tomio Yamamoto—had enough clout, earned by years of experience dealing with farm-related problems, for them to risk the wrath of farmers' groups and of Agriculture Ministry bureaucrats by raising the possibility of opening Japan's rice market.

In December 1992, at a press conference after his cabinet was reshuffled, Miyazawa hinted at the softening of Japan's negotiating stance: "We don't want to ruin the [Uruguay Round] negotiations and yet we don't want to ruin rice farming in Japan. How can we satisfy both goals?"[17] These remarks were Miyazawa's alone; they had not appeared in the press conference briefing materials that aides provided the prime minister.[18] His comments, however opaquely phrased, were taken to mean the Japanese side was on the brink of compromise on rice. According to insiders' accounts published in the press, Miyazawa had reached the conclusion that tariffication was "unavoidable" (*yamu o ezu*, the Japanese phrase always used when compromise is required).[19]

Behind Miyazawa's significant statement was the Japanese government's perception that it was in an untenable position in the multilateral negotiations. As long as the European Community and the United States remained at loggerheads on agricultural imports, Japanese leaders seemed quite content merely to watch from the sidelines, to let others take the heat for continued deadlock and the blame if the Uruguay Round talks collapsed. But the United States and the European Community had announced an agreement on November 24. Miyazawa was amazed that the French, who "disliked" the Americans, could have buckled under to Washington on the agricultural issue.[20]

In addition, Washington was strongly pressuring Tokyo to open its rice market. Japan's Agriculture minister, Makoto Tanabu, visited Washington in December 1992 to meet USTR Carla Hills and others to probe how

firmly U.S. trade officials were committed to their stance of "no exceptions." Finding them to be firmly committed, Tanabu returned to Tokyo,
where he reported his assessment to Miyazawa. At about the same time,
Miyazawa received a report on the multilateral situation from two of his
party's leading agricultural affairs politicians, Taichiro Okawara and
Kosuke Hori, who had just arrived back in Tokyo from Geneva. In addition, Miyazawa heard from his close friend Matsunaga that a settlement
was imminent in Geneva.[21] In light of information from these sources,
and anticipating a U.S.–European Community accommodation in
December 1992 that would have isolated Japan as the lone holdout on
agricultural imports, Miyazawa was now prepared to take decisive action.
His government, backed by ranking agricultural Diet members in his
party and top Agriculture Ministry bureaucrats, was ready—however
reluctantly—to compromise on the rice issue. Japanese leaders were
troubled by several future repercussions if Japan maintained its uncom-
promising posture on rice imports: the possibility that Japan would
"become isolated" *(koritsuka)* at the Uruguay Round; the likelihood that
Japan would become the scapegoat if the negotiations were to fail; and the
chance that the United States might retaliate in some fashion, threatening
other Japanese economic sectors and even the stability of the Japanese-
American relationship itself. These were not far-fetched concerns; they
seemed to be based on an accurate assessment of conditions at the multilateral level and of repeatedly expressed American expectations of Japan.

During this middle phase of the negotiations, the Japanese consensus
against rice imports gradually unraveled. The first major group to take a
more conciliatory line was Keizai doyukai, a liberal internationalist
business-world organization akin to the Committee for Economic Development in the United States. Certain noted Japanese economists followed,
echoing Keizai doyukai's support of a compromise solution to the rice problem. Then, in succession, moving slowly from left to right in the Japanese
political spectrum, others followed suit: the major newspapers; urban-
based political parties; the U.S.-oriented government ministries (first Gaimusho, then MITI); and the most influential big-business organization,
Keidanren (the Federation of Economic Organizations).

By the end of 1992, the once impregnable dike against imported rice was
about to give way. Only the party politicians from rural districts and

Agriculture Ministry bureaucrats still had fingers in the dike. As happened during the negotiations on orange imports, the bureaucrats at Agriculture began to bend, while Diet members representing rural districts remained steadfast in resisting any compromise. Their political goal was straightforward enough: to demonstrate their resolve by continuing to oppose rice imports until the last possible moment, convey to their constituents the "great efforts" they had exerted to avoid concessions, and let other politicians and government bureaucrats take the responsibility—and the blame—for accepting a negotiating defeat. Even the most die-hard opponents of tariffication were scrambling about in search of a face-saving solution as multilateral pressure at the Uruguay Round threatened to isolate Japan on the issue. Agriculture Ministry officials responded by seeking to negotiate the best deal possible under the circumstances. Once the ministerial fingers were pulled from the dike, the vote-conscious politicians seemed almost relieved to be able to surrender the issue of rice to the bureaucracy, permitting Agriculture officials to wield negotiating authority. By this point, the rice-import issue no longer was "whether or not" but "when" and "how much."

As it happened, however, and perhaps fortunately for the Japanese side, the confrontation between the European Community and the United States had not in fact ended in November. This gave Tokyo a respite, at least until the Clinton administration took office in January. Miyazawa's readiness to compromise on rice imports, albeit at the final hour, and his subsequent readiness to postpone taking action on the issue underline the extent to which the Japanese side's position was reactive, varying according to fluctuations in U.S. policy and in the circumstances at Geneva.

FINAL PHASE: THE SHIWAKU-O'MARA CONNECTION

The Bush years ended with a standoff on the subject of rice imports, with Washington standing firmly behind its no-exceptions position and Tokyo doggedly seeking preferential treatment on rice. The new administration's trade team, working against the backdrop of the looming deadline for wrapping up the Uruguay Round multilateral negotiations, moved aggressively—both in style and in substance—to resolve the rice issue.

The president himself was less confrontational, although no less determined, when he met Miyazawa at a bilateral summit on April 16, 1993. Miyazawa recited the standard Japanese script—that tariffication of rice would require changing the Food Control Law, which would be impossible. Instead of responding with the American no-exceptions argument, as Bush had done repeatedly, Clinton chose a more diplomatic response, so as to avoid jeopardizing the overall success of the Uruguay Round. In May a meeting of trade ministers from the United States, Canada, Japan, and the European Community agreed to open comprehensive trade negotiations in the fall, a decision that intensified pressure on Japan to face and resolve the rice problem.

An American initiative provided the catalyst for advancing the rice negotiations to the final stage. In June 1993, Charles J. O'Mara, chief negotiator in the Department of Agriculture, arranged a meeting with his counterpart in the Ministry of Agriculture, Jiro Shiwaku, who held the post of councilor (*shingikan,* a slot just slightly below bureau director on the Japanese bureaucratic ladder of status).[22] Shiwaku and others in the Agriculture Ministry believed that, with tariffication and free competition in the domestic Japanese rice market, rice grown in the United States would be at a serious disadvantage compared to rice grown in Thailand, where labor costs were much lower. Shiwaku thought, as had proved to be the case with wheat, that import quotas determined on a nation-by-nation basis would be more advantageous to the United States than would an open-market approach. Ministry of Agriculture officials also thought that the Clinton administration, being interested in results-oriented, managed trade rather than in demonstrating pious devotion to free trade ideology, would be receptive to applying the wheat precedent to resolution of the rice issue on a non-tariffication basis. Shiwaku ran this argument by the U.S. side, which listened. After all, thanks to a decade of preferential import treatment, compliments of the Ministry of Agriculture, half the wheat sold in Japan was grown in America.

The U.S. side did more than listen, however. In June 1993, O'Mara submitted a compromise draft proposal to Shiwaku that suggested deferring tariffication on rice for six years, during which period rice would be imported into Japan according to a "minimum-access" formula. According to the formula, tariffication of rice would not begin until the year 2000, after the six-year minimum-access period.[23] In an interview with the author, O'Mara confirmed the accuracy of reports published in the Japanese press regarding his private meetings with Shiwaku, including the fact that the overture was a U.S. initiative.

O'Mara's plan, which allowed Japan to avoid immediate tariffication of rice, was a welcome surprise to the Japanese team. "It was more than we expected," was the reaction of one delighted Japanese negotiator.[24]

In July, Agriculture Ministry officials assembled to review the O'Mara draft. The bureaucratic lineup and relatively receptive thinking of officials in the ministry continued even through the domestic political chaos of mid-1993, as defections and electoral losses brought the end of the thirty-eight-year reign of the LDP and the beginning of a series of multi-party coalition governments. Despite the cascade of domestic political events in Japan, these were the officials whose views mattered most in determining the Japanese side's negotiating position. They promptly decided to accept the American draft.

On the other hand, the LDP politicians ready to accept rice imports a year before, when their party was in power, had now become members of the opposition. Now they were unfettered by concerns about shouldering the burden, and the blame, associated with making a decision to open the rice market.

The American side was closely monitoring the internal political environment, with an eye to the implications these changes, particularly the Liberal Democrats' fall from power, would have on Japanese negotiating policy. Had the Liberal Democrats, the Americans wondered, altered their earlier stance? In early August, American trade officials invited Guzo Iwakura, a savvy agricultural affairs specialist and longtime party staff official, to Washington to learn the opposition party's thinking on the subject of rice. In the meeting, O'Mara asked Iwakura how the Liberal Democrats would respond to the draft proposal. "Even though we're the opposition party now, we'll respond by putting national interests first," was Iwakura's reassuring reply—which O'Mara and the Americans interpreted to mean the party would support, or at least not oppose, the compromise plan.[25]

The tide in favor of compromise was strengthened that same month, when, to compensate for a shortfall in Japan's domestic rice crop, the Japanese government decided to import rice from several countries on an emergency basis. These imports undermined even further Japan's adherence to the principle of national self-sufficiency in rice. Attempts by Japan's representatives to rationalize these as "one-time-only" purchases were unconvincing. Some Japanese leaders feared that, in the wake of the emergency rice imports, Japan would be criticized for hypocrisy and opportunism if it continued to stonewall on the compromise agreement.

As Japan commenced emergency imports, Ministry of Agriculture officials secretly approached the Rice Millers' Association (RMA). That meeting brought yet another surprise for the Japanese side, as RMA officers expressed their willingness to go along with the deferred-tariffication approach. In fact, following its discussion with the Agriculture Ministry representatives, the RMA sought U.S. Department of Agriculture guarantees on rice imports to Japan.

Thus, by the beginning of September the two sides had crafted the basis for a compromise agreement that seemed acceptable both to the most vociferous American lobbying protagonist and to the principal antagonists in the Japanese ministries and political parties. Meanwhile, the indefatigable Shiwaku continued to toil in the trenches on the details of an accord, for the most part side by side with his American counterpart, O'Mara. From September on, Shiwaku, who reportedly had "virtually complete" negotiating authority over the rice issue,[26] was engaged in discussions in Washington and Europe. He met secretly with O'Mara at a small hotel in France, using a rental car, but not using a pager or cellular phone. No record of these meetings appears in the Gaimusho records; only a small number of Agriculture Ministry officials were aware that the meetings were in progress.[27]

The Shiwaku-O'Mara meetings focused on several specific issues, including coming up with an acceptable translation for the key word *yuuyo*. Shiwaku balked at the English translation, "postponement" or "delay"; he favored more ambiguous language. In the end, the problem was averted through a circumlocution. The two officials also dealt with exactly how much rice could be imported during the six-year minimum-access period and with how to handle matters thereafter. The Dunkel draft had set forth a staggered percentage increase for rice imports, from 3 percent in the first year to 5 percent in the sixth year. Japan pushed for the Dunkel figures; the United States countered with percentages twice as high (6 to 10 percent over six years). In the end, the sides landed squarely in the middle, agreeing on a 4 to 8 percent formulation.[28]

His task virtually completed, Shiwaku returned to Tokyo on October 10. He and O'Mara had worked out a mutually satisfactory arrangement that achieved Washington's goal of accessing the Japanese rice market and Tokyo's goal of averting immediate tariffication. The final U.S.-Japan bilateral deal, which the major GATT nations would have to review and approve by the December 15 Uruguay Round deadline, stipulated that in exchange for raising (beyond the original Dunkel percentages) the amount of rice imported under the "minimum-access" formulation, Japan would be able to postpone tariffication until the year 2000. Thus, the U.S. initiative of mid-1993 (the O'Mara plan) had proved the breakthrough in the negotiations on rice, providing the Japanese side with a face-saving path of retreat. The negotiated deal had several pluses: it met the U.S. requirement that Japan start accepting rice imports; it allowed Japan to import only comparatively modest amounts of rice initially; it entailed a politically and economically manageable process of step-by-step increases in imports; it committed Japan to a rice-import structure that other rice-importing countries would follow; it seemed to meet other countries' expectations of Japan at the Uruguay Round; and it would, for a time, postpone resolution of the still politically contentious matter of rice tariffication.

The final compromise solution made sense, but would it survive the formidable political obstacles in Japan? Of the many obstacles to rice liberalization that Japanese officials and politicians had listed repeatedly before and during negotiations, several were rooted in hard political reality. One was the Diet resolution on self-sufficiency in rice, which remained in effect and which was taken seriously as a commitment. Another constraint stemmed from the long-term and unchanged public statements of many politicians and political parties opposing the importation of a single grain of rice. The chief obstacle to winning acceptance of the compromise draft, an obstacle that caused the premier to be "tied up in knots" (*ganji garame*, a Japanese phrase that describes being caught between a rock and a hard place),[29] was disagreement within his governing coalition serious enough to threaten its continuation in power. Prime Minister Morihiro Hosokawa's whopping 70 percent public support rating obscured his government's inner frailty; his popularity did not translate into the political clout to impose his will on opponents in his multiparty government, especially on a subject as touchy as rice. Hosokawa himself supported liberalization and had told associates that he would "open the rice market."[30] However, in a conversation with a top policy adviser in September, he had remarked that Japan should not liberalize rice without getting something in return: "If Japan can get conditions attached to liberalization, we should do so."[31]

MULTILATERAL PRESSURE

In mid-October GATT director general Peter Sutherland trekked to Tokyo, where he spent two exhausting days trying to convey to Japan's leaders the urgency of the imminent deadline for finishing up the Uruguay Round.[32] During his stay he conferred with bureaucrats and with Liberal Democrat and Socialist party leaders who, to an exasperated Sutherland, seemed determined just to state Japan's unrelenting opposition to rice imports and to recite from the well-rehearsed list of reasons for that opposition. Perhaps his background in Ireland as justice minister and in the EC establishment left him less familiar with Japanese-style arguments on the issue than were Americans. Sutherland reacted with surprise, and even astonishment, when the Japanese leaders he met seemed indifferent to the fact that agriculture was but one of more than a dozen major topics at the Uruguay Round. Two of the other topics were trade in services and intellectual property rights, which he expected to be of far greater concern to his Japanese hosts. Aside from leaders of Japan's powerful Keidanren, who were "the only people I could talk to," he told the press, "the only thing anyone seems interested in talking about is rice." "They seem to think rice imports mean the end of the world," he went on, "but they don't."[33]

Sutherland's comments had repercussions. For instance, once the outspoken Sutherland had left town, Hosokawa felt compelled to reassure the press, "I told him [Sutherland] Japan would not accept tariffication."[34]

Like many foreign observers and government officials who criticized Japan's one-dimensional negotiating performance at the Uruguay Round, Sutherland apparently failed to appreciate the extraordinary weight of the topic of rice liberalization in the Japanese mind. In the Japanese view, concluding the Uruguay Round would mean an avalanche of foreign rice into Japan. The Japanese newspapers skipped quickly over other Uruguay Round happenings to zero in on one question: What about rice? This preoccupation with a single and, to Japanese, nonnegotiable subject virtually ruled out objective policy debate on the topic. Rice liberalization was a taboo topic, even at the highest levels of the Japanese government, until negotiations neared completion.

Only by appreciating this Japanese outlook on the topic can one explain the otherwise baffling intensity of the Japanese side's efforts—at each stage and at both the bilateral and multilateral levels—to explain Japan's situation, gain special treatment for Japan's rice sector, and escape compromise on a matter of peripheral consequence to all but a few other governments.

THE FINAL, FINAL PHASE: SACRIFICING A SYMBOL TO SAVE THE SITUATION

The prime minister's defensive and evasive public statements stemmed from the tightrope he was walking in domestic politics. Caught between his own preferences and commitments and his die-hard political opponents, Hosokawa was frustrated and cautious. He also was pessimistic about the usefulness of continued Japanese stonewalling. He told one coalition party leader that Japan's merely saying "we oppose, we oppose" (hantai, hantai) "will not work."[35]

The hostile political and press backlash to reports of his remarks led Hosokawa to avoid comment on the subject. He fended off a barrage of questions on the Diet floor concerning rumored Japanese compromises with such comments as "Such reports haven't reached me," "You can't believe every story you hear," and "Diplomatic negotiations should be handled secretly."[36] However, former GATT secretary general Dunkel, in Tokyo for a conference, commented that there were no major differences between the secrecy-shrouded compromise plan and the original draft plan, a statement that encouraged the rumors that were circulating.[37]

Another Sutherland remark may have affected Japanese handling of negotiations during the final month of the process. In November, Minister of Agriculture Eishiro Hata decided to travel to Europe for a week of meetings with Sutherland and European Community trade officials.

His last-minute trip apparently was inspired by hopes of exploiting a possible opening signaled by an ambiguous remark Sutherland had made in October. While in Tokyo, Sutherland had confessed, "What I want is an agreement. As long as the involved countries agree, even if they want to say white is black, that's all right by me."[38]

Thus, even as the terms of the final agreement seemed settled, the Japanese side still was grasping at straws—in this case, Sutherland's remark —that might somehow improve the rice-related provisions of the accord. Whether or not Sutherland's ambiguous remark had actually prompted the minister's final-hour foray to the other side of the world, Hata's goal was perfectly clear from his own statements. "Having already swallowed the stick," he remarked ruefully, "we'll try to make it less painful."[39] By "less painful," Hata had in mind an improved deal for Japan, one that would postpone rice tariffication to some unspecified future time instead of beginning the process in the seventh year, as the compromise plan required.

In Tokyo, Hosokawa launched a preemptive strike against opponents of the compromise plan. Aware that a domestic backlash might jeopardize chances of an agreement, Hosokawa turned to two veteran Foreign Ministry officials, Yukio Sato and Hisashi Owada, who then dealt with Agriculture Ministry bureaucrats. Agriculture officials virtually never met with the prime minister himself at his residence over this period.[40]

Hosokawa's near-obsession with secrecy, and his worries that the rice problem might spill over to affect the U.S.-Japan relationship, spurred him to ask the Americans (through Ambassador Walter Mondale) not to make rice imports an issue at the upcoming Asia-Pacific Economic Cooperation (APEC) summit in Seattle. The U.S. side, appreciating Hosokawa's precarious position, apparently agreed to downplay the subject at the November summit;[41] the meeting went as expected, with the rice issue given the low-key treatment sought beforehand.

Hosokawa returned to Tokyo and began arrangements for a final round of consultations among his party allies in the coalition. His personal choice for undertaking this delicate task was Kazuo Ogura, chief of the Economic Bureau in the Foreign Ministry. Perhaps Ogura had instructions to be especially tight-lipped in his comments and especially narrow in his circle of briefing contacts. Perhaps not. In any case, he did not consult farm lobbying organizations. Moreover, his briefings to the politicians and officials he did meet revealed only information already published in the newspapers.

Hosokawa was certainly using his best spin-doctoring skills to obscure what had really been happening in the final stage of the negotiations on rice imports. Just a week before the Uruguay Round ended, Japanese government officials not only were denying reports of a compromise settlement but also were asserting that Tokyo was still engaged in final-hour attempts to improve rice-import terms. As late as December 9, days before conclusion of the Uruguay Round was announced, Hosokawa himself publicly denied reports of a final agreement.

The Japanese leader's denial strained credulity. One person who responded publicly about Hosokawa's statement was the ever-quotable GATT director. Sutherland, who was obviously aware of the facts, seemed unable to resist likening Hosokawa's remark to "calling white 'black.'"[42]

Nor did the prime minister's denial do anything to reassure skittish Japanese politicians. From that point until the December settlement, the frantic maneuverings of Japanese politicians did not stem from their concern with a foreign audience or with influencing the negotiations. Their target was their electoral constituents and party rivals. At the same time, no politician seemed willing to go up against the international situation (taisei) with Japan isolated in opposing a standard set by the international community.[43] The vast majority of Diet members of all parties were on record as having deemed rice imports to be inevitable. A sizable minority had declared rice tariffication to be unavoidable. These same politicians were now frantically scurrying about, seeking refuge from being held accountable for the reported Japanese concessions on rice.

Most politicians blamed the bureaucrats. Liberal Democratic politicians blamed the Hosokawa coalition—despite Iwakura's assurances to O'Mara and other American negotiators some months earlier that the Liberal Democrats would put the national interest first. In the crunch, it seemed, Iwakura's party colleagues were less interested in lending their support to a beleaguered prime minister than in jockeying for political advantage by pledging unaltered loyalty to the slogan "no foreign rice." Politicians hoped to demonstrate that they had exerted sufficiently "great efforts" and had tried their best, albeit in a losing cause. By the same token, the government leaders' ex post facto statements are best viewed as damage-control tactics to minimize the impact of what were—to Japanese minds—wholly unsatisfactory final terms. A mere handful of politicians stood behind Hosokawa (and the vaunted "national interest") and showed themselves willing to shoulder the risks and responsibilities associated with supporting the final agreement.

After seven tumultuous years of haggling Tokyo relented, and a settlement was agreed on that would—however grudgingly, incrementally, and slowly—end with the removal of all restrictions on imports of rice to Japan. In light of the bargaining record, it seems ironic that when announcing their decision to accept the final agreement, Japanese leaders explained the decision as motivated by Japanese devotion to free trade principles, dedication to the GATT process, and commitment to fulfilling their nation's responsibilities as a global economic power

CONCLUSION

What prompted Japanese concessions in this case? Japan tended to offer significant concessions only at the final stage and only when circumstances surrounding negotiations had become heavily politicized and the Japanese side had come to see itself as having no choice but to compromise.

One significant final-stage source of pressure to concede was multilateral. If Japan was the only country standing in the way of reaching unanimous agreement at the Uruguay Round, Japan feared it would be isolated and blamed for the collapse of the talks. Another, more potent, final-stage source of pressure was bilateral, namely, Japanese fears of American retaliation for noncompliance with its proposals and the consequent threat to other, economically more significant, sectors of the Japanese economy. The Japanese were apparently relieved when Washington offered in 1993 to postpone tariffication of rice imports until 2000, and their sense of relief seems to have made the Japanese side more willing to accept earlier American proposals it had rejected.

In light of the reasons why the Japanese side accepted the minimum-access and deferred-tariffication formula, it probably made little, if any, difference which party or coalition of parties happened to be in government in Japan when the final-stage decisions were reached in the fall of 1993. As it was, Hosokawa's government justified final concessions on the grounds that they permitted agreement with better terms than those the other side had been demanding earlier.

As noted at the outset of this chapter, the negotiations on rice high-lighted several elements of the "coping" approach that runs throughout Japanese diplomacy, both at the loftier plateau of policymaking and down in the trenches at the level of direct negotiations. Three elements in par-ticular were much in evidence: a desire to avoid or minimize the scope of negotiations; an inability to move forward until a consensus has been built at home; and an overarching reactive, or defensive, posture.

Issue Avoidance and Issue Minimization

The Japanese government's dearest wish in the negotiations over rice imports (and, indeed, orange imports) was not to enter into negotiations in the first place. In part, this desire was prompted by concrete political realities: farmers, their political representatives and allies, and the public at large all opposed the importation of rice. Partly, though, the desire to avoid discussing the issue altogether can be seen as a reflection of a dis-tinctly Japanese view of negotiations. Judging from Japanese commentary on the topic, negotiation is seen not as a legitimate clash of opposing points of view but as a failure of the consensus-building process. Japanese negotiation is not really negotiation as Westerners understand it but rather the rubber-stamping of agreements already reached after hearing and taking into account all relevant views. Meetings merely legitimize consensus-based decisions.

On the international stage, negotiation represents a failure on the part of the Japanese to communicate their point of view, which if communi-cated properly would be understood as valid and accepted by the negoti-ating counterpart. If an impasse is reached, it is reached because the other side has not understood Japan's point of view or the constraints under which Japan is laboring. Hence, the Japanese engage in behavior that to a Western audience can seem almost bizarre: round after round of delega-tions coming from Japan to hurl themselves against foreign resistance, convinced that the issue can be dealt with merely by communicating Japan's point of view.

In the case of rice, Japan used numerous techniques to block or defer consideration of what, to the Japanese side, were subjects that did not belong on either bilateral or multilateral agendas. Once avoidance efforts had failed, the Japanese side sought to reduce the scope and content of the compromises required to resolve the issues. These issue-avoidance and -minimization techniques included

❖ repeatedly emphasizing and explaining that the subject of rice was off-limits for discussion;

❖ gaining prior understandings or promises (in personal meetings with U.S. officials) that rice would be off-limits or that, if the subject was discussed, Japan would receive exceptional, special, or preferential treatment;

❖ seeking to mutlilateralize negotiations in the hope of sidestepping U.S. demands and averting action;

❖ adopting a watch-and-wait posture at the multilateral level; and

❖ offering minor concessions and then postponing further compromise until the U.S. response had been received and assessed.

Consensus Building

Decision making in Japan's political culture requires expending enormous energy and time in consensus building. Only by extensive discussions, behind-the-scenes consultations, and formal and informal conferences can a viable decision be arranged. According to Japanese norms of politics, all relevant opinions must be heard and taken into consideration when reaching policy decisions. This requirement is demanding at the best of times; in the case of rice imports, a subject with a very high public and political profile, the process of building consensus was extremely problematic and shaped Japanese bargaining style in various ways.

In the first place, even when Japan's prime minister and other high-ranking ministers, including the minister of agriculture, had come to accept the inevitability of allowing U.S. rice into Japan, Japanese negotiators could not conclude a deal until a critical mass of key politicians and senior ministerial officials were persuaded to agree to the import of foreign rice. Hosokawa's efforts to build a political consensus were Herculean, but they did not bear fruit until Japan felt tremendous bilateral and multilateral pressure to compromise. Until the last, the Japanese government kept looking for some sign of flexibility within the American side that might permit Japan to strike a better deal—that is, a deal around which it would be easier to rally domestic support.

In the second place, various Japanese official and nonofficial actors used external pressure—real, imagined, expected, and typically American—to generate added support at home for policies they personally espoused but might not have been able to accomplish without a dash of *gaiatsu*. The many missions, delegations, and personal envoys to the United States were dispatched for domestic political reasons. These visits facilitated the softening of the Japanese stance and thus were a critical part of the process of reaching final agreements.

Third, the Japanese leadership had to take into account—and if possible placate—not only government officials and the fractious members of Hosa-kawa's ruling coalition but also powerful private groups such as Keidanren. In this respect, the Japanese government shared much the same problem as the American government. Indeed, the high level of involvement of nonofficial actors on both sides reflects the diversity, complexity, and intensely interrelated quality of relationships between the two societies. Both sides' official positions were shaped by these factors. For instance, Japanese negotiators' *nemawashi* efforts included a visit to the offices of the Rice Millers' Association to test the waters on the final compromise plan.

Fourth, the Japanese side typically took two to three months to prepare and present its positions at the negotiating table. The lengthy response time stemmed not from intentional delaying or stalling tactics by the Japanese side but from the snail-like pace of building lowest-common-denominator consensus among all parties having a stake in the issues being considered. The escalation of U.S. demands clearly imposed added hardships on this domestic decision-making process, making it even more time-consuming.

Fifth, the delicate business of consensus building can easily be upset by an untimely leak of sensitive information. And such leaks are an ever-present danger, given the insatiable appetite of the Japanese press for scoops and information. If details of private discussions (for instance, the Shiwaku-O'Mara conversations during 1993) can be kept from the press, the domestic decision-making process is smoothed considerably, which, in turn, may help produce a politically sustainable final agreement. Given the fiercely combative political environment and a scoop-driven army of Japanese journalists, Hosokawa (like any Japanese leader) had to perform a balancing act. On the one hand, his secretive approach seems to have allowed the O'Mara-Shiwaku talks to achieve results that publicity might have made impossible. On the other hand, keeping details of the final compromise plan from the public (and some domestic parties) even after the deal had been negotiated left him vulnerable to political attack when the terms of the final agreement became known.

The United States Plays Offense, Japan Plays Defense

The U.S. side was the driving force throughout the negotiations. Washington established the bargaining agenda, issued direct and indirect threats, undertook the significant initiatives, set the deadlines, and, at the multilateral level, acted to mobilize other governments to buttress its negotiating stance vis-à-vis Japan.

In sharp contrast, the Japanese played a defensive role: Japanese negotiators did not frame the initial bargaining agenda but reacted within the framework of a U.S.-dominated agenda and process. Japan's proposals were counterproposals. Its conditions were strings attached to the acceptance of American demands. Its bargaining game plan was executed on an American playing field—with an American rule book, American referees, an American scorekeeper, and an American crew adjusting the height of the goalposts. No matter at what level negotiations took place—bilateral, multilateral, or bilateral within multilateral *(maruchi-bi)*—the policies, approach, and behavior of Japanese negotiators were conditioned by Japan's defensive position.

This is not to say the Japanese were passive, for they were actively engaged in the bargaining process. Their active involvement, however, took place in an externally defined context. Their initiatives were not designed to replace or fundamentally alter the existing, made-in-America negotiating agenda.

Sudden changes in that agenda, or in the manner in which it was presented, understandably elicited complaints from the Japanese side. Throughout the course of the negotiations, Japanese negotiators and officials complained often—and usually with good reason—about Washington's negotiating conduct. Alleged American shortcomings included

❖ unexplained, sudden escalation of demands, such as Eagleburger's announcement that partial access was not enough and only tariffication would do;

❖ discrepancies between U.S. positions expressed at the multilateral level and those set forth in bilateral meetings;

❖ violation of previous Japanese-U.S. understandings or promises, such as Yeutter's assurance that the United States would not press Japan to liberalize its rice market;

❖ excessive use of pressure and threats; and

❖ repeated submission of demands that the American side knew were off-limits—that is, clearly beyond Japan's maximum concessionary range, such as the demand for tariffication at a time when it was not feasible to change the Food Control Law.

Such American behavior had a particularly striking impact on the Japanese side's conduct of the negotiations, precisely because Japan's bargaining menu was provided by the United States. When the U.S. side changed or added items to the agenda, the existing Japanese internal consensus disintegrated. Tokyo then had to arrange a fresh consensus, more or less from scratch, on the basis of the latest U.S. plan.

The Japanese also faced difficulties from what they saw as extravagant U.S. demands. Whether or not the United States artificially inflated its demands, the later withdrawal of Eagleburger's demand for rapid tariffication seems to have affected the bargaining process (by hastening settlement between the sides) and the final outcome (by improving the final terms for the U.S. side). However loudly and often Japanese officials cried foul over this violation of bargaining norms by the Americans, from the U.S. perspective the tactic (if it was, in fact, intentional) of submitting and then retracting especially harsh conditions was an effective tool. Why the American ploy worked so well is explained by Japan's place in a fundamentally defensive bargaining structure and by the Japanese side's view of its position within that framework as weak, vulnerable, and necessarily reactive.

Japanese perceptions of Japan as a have-not country are deeply embedded. Many Japanese see their country as handicapped among nations, isolated geographically, virtually without natural resources, with scarce arable land, whose economic survival—let alone its prosperity—requires open access to other countries' markets and whose national security depends on sustaining a military alliance with a once-hated foe. In Japanese eyes, the risks of diplomatic and negotiating activism far outweigh the possible benefits. Japanese commentators likened the American campaign to export rice into Japan to Commodore Perry's mid-nineteenth-century opening of Japan to the West or the Americanization of Japan during the U.S. Occupation. From the Japanese perspective, every grain of foreign rice was a bullet aimed at the cultural heart of Japan.

3

THE FSX AIRCRAFT NEGOTIATIONS, 1985–89

Michael Blaker

The continued presence of U.S. troops in Japan beyond the end of the Occupation in 1952 seemed to many Japanese to be a form of U.S. retribution for Pearl Harbor and the ensuing war. There was thus strong ambivalence about the continued security alliance with the United States, reflected in perennial press reports critical of the U.S. military presence and in protests that peaked in 1959–60 and in 1969. The Japanese government seems not to have encouraged the protests but it did tolerate them, aware that they strengthened its weak bargaining position in negotiations with the United States over the two countries' military alliance and the provision of bases and base support for U.S. troops stationed in Japan.

After the U.S.-Japan Security Alliance was renewed in 1969, opposition to it gradually diminished. Although many quiet discussions were held about the extent of the bases and Japanese support, the actual alliance grew fairly steady. The security relationship was managed largely by the Japanese Ministry of Foreign Affairs and by the U.S. Departments of Defense and State. Bureaucrats on both sides could manage the relationship in a relatively harmonious manner, given the broad political support they received from their governments on the issue. The military establishment in both countries also supported the security alliance. The U.S. Department of Defense considered the alliance very helpful to U.S. global strategy, and the Japanese Defense Agency (JDA) also believed it vital to maintain the alliance. As a consequence, bilateral discussions on security proceeded relatively smoothly through the 1970s and 1980s.

Bilateral discussions on trade were another matter entirely. As we have seen in the preceding two chapters, negotiations over U.S. access to

Japanese markets for agricultural products were usually protracted, often acrimonious, and sometimes painful, especially for the Japanese side. Tensions and hostility were even more acute in negotiations over industrial imports and exports, especially automobiles and high technology, and especially in the late 1980s and early 1990s. The rise in the value of the Japanese yen from the mid-1980s and the extraordinary Japanese economic growth enabled the Japanese to buy up U.S. properties and companies in addition to expanding their own industrial capacity. By 1985, the American trade deficit with Japan was a whopping $59 billion. This led to great concern within the U.S. business community and to increasing pressure from U.S. negotiators to open the Japanese markets.

It is against this backdrop that we must see the negotiations over proposals for Japan to develop and build its own fighter aircraft. The aircraft would be a close-support fighter, known as Fighter Support, Experimental (FSX). The development of a new, state-of-the-art fighter jet was, of course, a security matter—and the U.S.-Japanese security relationship was thought to be, by and large, manageable. However, the FSX project was equally clearly also a trade matter—if Japan built its own plane, it would further strengthen its high-tech industry while depriving the U.S. aerospace industry of sales to Japan—and the U.S.-Japanese trade relationship was decidedly acrimonious. This conflation of security and economic issues might perhaps have produced negotiations in which harmony and acrimony balanced each other. It did not. Instead, acrimony predominated, accentuated by nationalistic resentment on both sides.

In all, the negotiations ran from the mid-1980s until the early 1990s, with the FSX development project finally entering the prototype production phase in 1993. In this chapter, however, we focus on the period from 1986, when negotiations began, until April 1989, when Japan and the United States "clarified" an agreement originally reached in November 1988. Thereafter, the issue continued to arouse considerable political heat in both countries, with members of the U.S. Congress denouncing what they saw as a "giveaway" of advanced aerospace technology to America's most relentless economic rival and Japanese politicians and media expressing fury and frustration at the Bush administration's insistence on further clarifications of the agreement.[1] But by the spring of 1989 the overall shape of the FSX agreement had been established, and bilateral discussion would thereafter center on financial and technical—albeit politically sensitive—issues, not on competing visions of Japan's role within the U.S.-Japan alliance.

HISTORICAL BACKGROUND

Beginning in the late 1960s, Japanese defense planners began to consider seriously the idea of a totally Japanese-made close-support fighter jet. Germinating in the Japanese aircraft industry, the seeds of the idea finally burst through the surface in the form of government memoranda during the 1970s. The idea swiftly took root, for the soil was fertile: a vibrant, expanding economy; a Japanese military less fettered by the legacy of Japanese militarism and imperialism; closer security links with the United States after the Soviet incursion into Afghanistan; and rising nationalism. Japan was eager to develop its aerospace industry, and domestic production of a state-of-the-art fighter would surely advance that goal. Although Japan still lacked the technological expertise to produce such a fighter, many in Japan's military and industrial sectors were confident that such skills could be quickly acquired once the fighter project had been launched.

The catalyst that permitted the advocates of a Japanese-made fighter to attract attention and support came from the United States, in the form of U.S. trade policies aimed at opening the Japanese market to foreign products and services, along with what Japanese security and defense specialists saw as an American attempt to retard Japanese technological growth by "black boxing" more and more technology to Japan.

As the 1980s advanced, Japanese resolve stiffened. The last of the seventy-seven domestically produced F-1s rolled off the Nagoya facility of Mitsubishi Heavy Industries (MHI) on March 9, 1987. For Japanese advocates of an indigenously manufactured fighter, the once-remote possibility suddenly became an inviting opportunity as the time neared to replace the aging F-1s in Japan's Air Self-Defense Force with a new generation of aircraft. Japan's top aerospace firms—backed by JDA officials, conservative, defense-oriented politicians, and like-minded bureaucrats at the Ministry of International Trade and Industry (MITI)—wanted a close-support fighter that would be designed and built in Japan. A consortium of aerospace firms led by MHI hoped to manufacture the "Rising Sun" jet.

Despite the enthusiastic and growing support in the mid-1980s for a Japanese-built fighter, this was but one of three options facing the Japanese government. There were two alternatives to a Rising Sun fighter: purchase of an off-the-shelf American fighter or manufacture of a fighter under license from a selected American firm with a Japanese company as prime contractor. As of January 1985, the government had announced no decision on the subject.[2] Many Americans, however, suspected that the Japanese government was already privately, if not publicly, committed to the Rising Sun option.

EARLY PHASE

In the lead-up to the negotiations on the FSX, the U.S. government was under pressure from the Departments of State and Commerce, members of Congress increasingly concerned by the rising U.S. trade deficit with Japan, and defense industry lobbyists from two leading aerospace firms—McDonnell Douglas and General Dynamics. These pressures combined to produce what was at that stage an essentially negative goal: namely, to thwart an apparently advanced and ambitious plan by the Japanese to build their own fighter. The Pentagon was less wary and less distrustful.

In June 1985 Secretary of Defense Caspar Weinberger broached the matter with his Japanese counterpart, JDA chief Koichi Kato, at a U.S.-Japan defense summit meeting in Hawaii. Weinberger's approach was deliberately restrained—an attempt to apply pressure by nonpressure. This low-key approach appears to have left the Japanese with the impression that Washington would accept a Japanese-made FSX. Kato "appreciated" Weinberger's restrained approach but was noncommittal about the Japanese stance on the FSX.[3] He stated that a made-in-Japan FSX was just one Japanese option, backed by industry and some bureaucrats and politicians, but that no final decision had been reached in Tokyo.

Later that summer the Japanese side realized it had misread the American position when U.S. officials urged Japan to agree to cooperative development of the FSX. What the American representatives had not stated clearly earlier was that the then-prevailing American mood ruled out a purely Japanese-made FSX—indeed, the preferred American option was outright purchase of a U.S.-built aircraft. As before, when queried on their thinking, Japanese spokesmen simply repeated their previous explanation that a wholly Japanese-built FSX was "merely one" of Tokyo's options. (One might argue that not choosing between options was in itself another Japanese option: that of keeping its options open.)

Over the summer and fall of 1985, the "merely one" option won growing support in the Japanese defense community, culminating in a report rejecting the idea of a U.S.-built fighter. According to the report, a Japanese-made aircraft would be less costly, more compatible with Japan's mission requirements, and technologically more advanced than a U.S.-built airplane.

Had the Japanese acted swiftly and decisively before the summer of 1985 to develop the FSX on their own, they might well have launched the project successfully. The American side was in disarray, with no coherent, unified policy position on the subject. Furthermore, various negative factors that shaped the course of the negotiations had yet to surface—an increasingly intrusive Congress; the emergence of an activist, hard-line Commerce Department; wrangling over the Strategic Defense Initiative; and the tempestuous "Toshiba scandal."[4]

For their part, the Japanese obviously were unaware that they had such a window of opportunity or that the window would soon slam shut. Instead, the Japanese government reached an important nondecision on FSX. A final decision on FSX was deferred to March 1986 and then postponed for one to two years.

Why was the decision deferred? Apparently advocates of Japanese autonomous production met stiff resistance from certain key actors, notably the Foreign Ministry, whose senior officials tended to weigh every policy option against a single standard—how it would affect the Japanese-American relationship. Top-level Foreign Ministry bureaucrats feared that a Japanese-made FSX, by raising the specter of a militarily assertive Japan, would damage that relationship.

In January 1986, fully six months after the two sides began negotiations on FSX, the United States proposed "co-development" of the new fighter. This belated U.S. proposal was submitted "unofficially."

By the time of the Tokyo Summit in May 1986, Prime Minister Yasuhiro Nakasone and other leading politicians in the ruling Liberal Democratic Party had become engaged in the FSX process. These top politicians, like the Foreign Ministry diplomats, viewed the FSX issue through the lens of the U.S.-Japan alliance. To these political leaders, keeping the relationship with the United States on an even keel took precedence over insisting that the production of a hundred or so fighter jets be done in Japan.

In July 1986 the Japanese side, in what Tokyo called "a conciliatory gesture," agreed to add joint development of a U.S. fighter to its formal list of FSX possibilities. The Japanese also "agreed to consider" new U.S. design proposals in contractor meetings. As the year progressed, Weinberger continued to press Tokyo to abandon the idea of indigenous production of the FSX, laying particular emphasis on growing congressional opposition to the project. In December 1986, the JDA, until then the most ardent advocate of autonomous production of the FSX in the government, officially reconsidered the Rising Sun fighter option.

After an initial period of skirmishing by each side, the Americans seemed to have the advantage. U.S. negotiators had apparently convinced the Japanese to revamp their options list, dropping purely domestic development and adding joint development. The newly added alternative was to become the principal—and stickiest—topic for bargaining during the next phase of negotiations.

Japan's negotiating approach during the initial stage was thoroughly defensive and armored in ambiguity. Time and again, Japanese officials balked at offering clear-cut statements of policy. The Japanese side, which not only was noncommittal but also had deferred its own decision on FSX, was content to remain rather aloof from the process, requesting additional information from the American government and aerospace companies. Letters also were sent requesting briefings by U.S. contractors. Envoys, teams of experts, and fact-finding missions were dispatched to the United States (and Europe) to explain the Japanese position and obtain more information. One such mission, led by Ryozo Tsutsui, director general of the Air Staff of the FSX Program Office, backfired badly. Abandoning the noncommittal approach adopted by other Japanese officials, Tsutsui bluntly declared to Pentagon officials that Japan planned to go it alone on production of the FSX. When asked to consider alternative production techniques, Tsutsui refused and took his delegation back to Japan. Japanese officials grossly misinterpreted the outcome of the mission, believing that Japan had been given a green light by the United States to proceed with a domestically produced FSX. In reality, the Tsutsui mission cemented a working-level consensus in the U.S. government against a Japan-made FSX. Even when Japanese delegations carried a more conciliatory message, they also managed to rile the Americans by insisting on various restrictions—for instance, withholding information on Japanese technology relevant to the proposed project.

MIDDLE PHASE

The pressure-response pattern of U.S.-Japanese bargaining during the early phase of negotiations would be replayed at each subsequent stage. By the end of 1986, negotiations on the FSX project were more emotionally charged. Hard-liners were centrally engaged in the process; U.S. industry lobbying efforts in Congress and sales promotions to the Japanese had become more intense; and FSX became increasingly linked to other subjects in the wake of two explosive incidents, the Toshiba scandal and the semiconductor dumping case.[5] This phase of the FSX negotiations started with discussions of joint development and ended with the Japanese agreeing, in effect, to pick an American plane.

In January 1987, Seiki Nishihiro, chief of defense policy in the JDA, met with Kevin Kearns from the U.S. embassy. The JDA, he told Kearns, "has put off a decision on the FSX for a year. But its budget planning for next fiscal year is based on a Japanese-made aircraft."[6] Nishihiro, who opposed domestic development of the FSX, seems to have been signaling the United States to act so as to preempt this Japanese budgetary decision.

If Nishihiro was indeed inviting American *gaiatsu* to help him bring reluctant Japanese officials into line with his own thinking on FSX, he had picked the right listener. Shortly after his appointment, Kearns had been struck by the pro-Japanese outlook among embassy staffers, and he coined the label Chrysanthemum Club to describe officials he considered interested more in maintaining U.S.-Japanese relations on an even keel than in protecting U.S. national interests. He feared that Japan was embarking on a militaristic path, and he had written a memo questioning whether the embassy was representing U.S. national interests adequately.

Kearns now prepared a long telegram about his meeting with Nishihiro and sent it to his superiors at the Department of Defense.

The Japanese were not unified on FSX. The Japanese aircraft industry was still committed to the Rising Sun option, but many within the upper echelons of the Japanese government had come to regard a domestically produced FSX as all but impossible. This division of opinion soon became apparent. On February 15, 1987, the *Nihon keizai shimbun* reported that a number of firms (including MHI, Fuji Heavy Industries, Ishikawajima, and Mitsubishi Electric) had formed a coalition whose goal was to undermine American dominance over the project and to pursue independent development. The consortium reportedly planned to go ahead with manufacture of a Rising Sun aircraft at MHI's Nagoya production facility and had prepared an autonomous production draft for submission to the JDA in March. The Japanese government did not welcome MHI's formation of the consortium. According to Omura Hitoshi, the man responsible for contractors in the JDA, the *Nihon keizai shimbun* "article is a news article, and MHI and the others in the coalition ought to know that their autonomous production proposal is politically impossible. So the industry coalition is merely a demonstration, an effort to gain an edge when negotiations begin with the United States for joint development."[7]

At a meeting of the U.S.-Japan security subcommittee in Hawaii, Richard Armitage, the U.S. assistant secretary of defense for international security affairs, presented an "unofficial" American proposal for joint development of the FSX fighter based on one of two U.S. aircraft, the McDonnell Douglas F-18 and the General Dynamics F-16. In a concession, he agreed to have a Japanese firm serve as the prime project contractor. Armitage had a stick as well as a carrot: he warned the Japanese that some Congress members were beginning to link trade friction to security issues, including the question of the FSX.

How right he was! Early in March 1987, Senator John Danforth sent a letter to the Reagan administration calling for Japan to purchase a U.S. fighter to help the American bilateral trade deficit with Japan. At about the same time Secretary of State George Schultz talked with Prime Minister Nakasone in Tokyo. Meanwhile, American aircraft companies began to train their heavy promotional artillery squarely in Japan's direction. Sales teams from McDonnell Douglas and General Dynamics visited Japan at the end of March.

As these events were unfolding, a delegation of American aircraft contractors, headed by Deputy Assistant Under Secretary of Defense Gerald Sullivan, spent half of April in Tokyo, where they met with the Japanese on FSX. Ostensibly there to exchange information with the Japanese, Sullivan's team had other items on their agenda: to call what they saw as a Japanese bluff on the superiority of Japan's technology and to go over the heads of Japanese working-level technocrats to reach the topmost echelons of political authority in the JDA. This approach seems to have worked. Yuko Kurihara, the director of the JDA, made plain to several high-ranking JDA officials who still advocated the Rising Sun fighter that the Japanese-led development option was no longer politically feasible.

Sullivan's mission quickened the tempo of the talks on both sides of the Pacific. The week after the team returned, Senators Bob Dole, Lloyd Bentsen, and Robert Byrd wrote Nakasone, strongly urging him to have Japan drop the idea of autonomous development of the FSX. And at the bilateral summit in Washington, D.C., in April, although President Reagan did not raise FSX with Nakasone, several senators, including Danforth, did. Tokyo dispatched a special envoy to Washington with the message that, as a sign of Japanese goodwill, Japan would consider purchase of a U.S.-built aircraft for the FSX.

In May the Toshiba incident erupted, enmeshing FSX and all Japanese-American issues in its tangled web. The next month, in a meeting with his Japanese counterpart, Nishihiro, Armitage upped the ante, warning that should Japan choose not to accept the American proposals on FSX, a complete reordering of the U.S.-Japan alliance might occur. Nishihiro duly reported this to his boss, Kurihara, who responded by telling Nishihiro that "the situation had changed" and that there was no need to rush to judgment on the subject of the FSX.

At the Okura Hotel in Tokyo on June 29, 1987, in a meeting with Weinberger and Armitage, Kurihara presented a fallback initiative—joint development of an entirely new aircraft. Weinberger responded coldly, rejecting Kurihara's proposal.

Events over the summer intensified the crisis. The Senate in a 97–0 vote urged Japan to buy an American aircraft off the shelf. Another Japanese mission organized by MHI was dispatched to the United States to press for a larger share of Japanese domestic production. Nakasone, under intense pressure to resolve the escalating crisis, stated that Japan was likely to accede to U.S. requests on FSX. To ease the rising tension, shortly after Nakasone made his comments, the Japanese government apparently reached a final decision to abandon autonomous production of the FSX and to base the new aircraft on an existing American-made fighter. In reaching this decision, Tokyo removed the F-18 from the list of candidate aircraft and pledged to select by October 20 one of two remaining candidates, the F-16 or the McDonnell Douglas F-15, as the basis for the FSX.

Early in October, at a meeting in Washington, Weinberger and Kurihara reached a preliminary agreement: the FSX would be based on a "lightly modified" version of one of the two airplanes. The two contending contractors, General Dynamics and McDonnell Douglas, then intensified their respective sales campaigns to the Japanese. Shortly thereafter, the Japanese government announced its choice: General Dynamics' F-16 Falcon.

After two and a half years, it seemed that the Department of Defense —aided by an obstreperous Congress, several incendiary public scandals, and doggedly persistent American negotiating pressure—had managed to wear down the Japanese side, which had retreated from the Rising Sun fighter to joint development of an all-new fighter to "joint development" of an existing American aircraft.

The issue, at last, was settled. Or was it? Despite political agreement, serious ambiguities remained.

PENULTIMATE PHASE

The next phase—which, contrary to expectations, turned out not to be the final phase—of the FSX negotiations involved bargaining at two levels. The first was government-to-government negotiations on an acceptable framework for joint development of the F-16–based FSX, a framework that would be laid out in a memorandum of understanding (MOU). The second was negotiations between General Dynamics and its counterpart Japanese aerospace companies.

Sticky issues had been glossed over previously. The ambiguities of the agreement immediately became apparent when U.S. industry teams visited Tokyo in October 1987 to tackle the matter of structuring the project, and in particular to decide the relative work share of the two sides in the project. The U.S. side raised the issue for the first time in these exchanges. To its surprise, the Japanese responded with a detailed draft proposal. The document, which designated a Japanese firm as prime contractor, contained many items that were unacceptable to the United States, such as unrestricted transfer to Japan of data and technology related to the F-16; American access to Japanese technology only on a case-by-case basis; all development work to be performed in Japan; and all program-related research and development (R&D) funds to be spent in Japan. The proposal mentioned nothing about the production phase.

According to RAND analyst Mark Lorell, this Japanese document demonstrates that even at this stage Japan was planning to transform the "collaborative" FSX into an essentially indigenous project, with only "formal" or "token" assistance from U.S. industry.[8] The American side spurned the Japanese proposal and, after a single day of talks, returned to the United States. The tough American reaction, however, had forced JDA officials to consult immediately with the Foreign Ministry and others. The Japanese side then agreed to reconsider and to submit a revised proposal at a meeting scheduled for a month later in Washington.

Japan's proposal had placed the American side on the defensive, a highly unusual position in its bilateral negotiations with Japan. Over the next few weeks, the U.S. team worked hard to patch together some semblance of a coherent counterproposal. The Japanese side's preparations involved more than revamping its proposal. Led by M. Yamamoto of the JDA's Equipment Bureau, Japan's FSX team was deliberating exhaustively on bargaining tactics. Yamamoto recognized that the American side did not have a unified policy or carefully worked-out tactics for negotiating on FSX. He reasoned that a hard-line Japanese stance, which included stonewalling each and every U.S. proposal, was the most promising way to exploit the vulnerable American position. Yamamoto's bargaining tactics were designed with one goal in mind: to take the F-16, study it, extract its technology, and convert it into a new Japanese fighter.[9] As it turned out, however, this approach was ultimately to fail, chiefly because other events diminished the relative importance of the FSX issue and persuaded the Japanese government to settle the matter on U.S. terms.

When the two sides met in Washington, the American team insisted on a government-to-government accord prior to an industry-level agreement

"Let's be buddies from now on, shall we?"

Yomiuri shimbun, May 1, 1989. Cartoon by Makino Shuichi. Reproduced with permission.

between manufacturing firms. This government-to-government agreement would specify a joint oversight committee and specific work-share percentages for development and for production, and it would guarantee the flow of technology back to the United States without cost. The Americans were prepared to accede to MHI serving as the prime project contractor. With regard to work share, the American side proposed 40 percent for the United States and 60 percent for Japan on development, and 30:70 percent on production.[10] The U.S. side also insisted that a full-fledged memorandum of understanding was needed. Washington informed Tokyo that the U.S. side would prepare the draft MOU and submit it to the Japanese early in 1988.

In February 1988 the American team forwarded a draft MOU to the JDA. Initially, Yamamoto flatly rejected the U.S. plan and countered with a proposal to give 100 percent of both development and production to Japanese companies. Thereafter, however, the Japanese appear to have switched tactics from outright rejection to a somewhat more subtle but (for the Americans) no less frustrating approach—summed up in the Japanese saying *soron sansei, kakuron hantai*, meaning to "agree in principle but disagree on the details." Over the next three months the two sides engaged in a bruising battle over details and percentages.

On June 3, 1988, Secretary of Defense Frank Carlucci and JDA chief Tsutomu Kawara met in Tokyo and agreed on figures for both development and production: 40 percent for the United States on development and 30 percent on production—just as the Americans had earlier proposed. Washington hailed the agreement as a "major victory." However, Kawara had yet to arrange the domestic consensus that would legitimize the agreement. Achieving that consensus took another six months, with the main obstacle this time being the Foreign Ministry. Finally, on November 29, Japanese foreign minister Sosuke Uno and U.S. ambassador Mike Mansfield reached agreement in the form of an MOU. Among other things, the MOU stipulated that the new aircraft would be a modification of the F-16C; the JDA would plan and manage the project and bear the cost of development; the prime contractor would be a Japanese company, with American companies participating as subcontractors; the precise allocation of tasks between the two countries would be determined later and would be based on cost-effectiveness; the U.S. side would provide the Japanese side with all pertinent technical data on the F-16C; and the Japanese side would provide the U.S. side with all pertinent data on derived technologies created during the development phase.[11] Bargaining over the MOU had been, as one Japanese observer put it, a "dogfight."[12]

Industry-level negotiations were still ensnared in bureaucratic turf-related squabbling *(nawabari arusoi)* among officials at MITI, the Foreign Ministry, and the JDA. Not until December 23, 1988, was the MHI proposal given to the U.S. side.

FINAL PHASE

If the Japanese thought that the MOU signed on November 29 would mean an end to negotiations and the beginning of joint development of the new aircraft, they were to be disappointed. January 1989 saw the installation of a new U.S. president and administration and the onset of a process of reevaluation of the November agreement.

Officials at the Pentagon had seen no need to inform the U.S. Department of Commerce about the MOU. Thus, when word of the agreement leaked out, Commerce officials, and especially the hard-liners toward Japan who came to dominate discussions of the FSX issue, were very unhappy at having been left out of the loop and protested vigorously to their colleagues in the Department of Defense. FSX was about to become a convenient vehicle for Commerce to demonstrate its clout on subjects related to military technology.

In February 1989, President George Bush and National Security Advisor Brent Scowcroft discussed the MOU at a heated meeting at the White House. There was a split between, on the one side, Commerce and the White House science adviser, Jack Simon, and, on the other side, the Departments of State and Defense. Carl Jackson, an assistant to Armitage and Bush's point man on East Asian affairs at the White House, was instructed to work out a unified U.S. position on FSX. To do that, he prepared a twenty-five-point questionnaire that he sent out to the relevant departments on February 5.

On February 10 and 14, two more interagency meetings were held, but no definitive conclusion was reached on FSX. The decision was made to go ahead and submit the November 1988 agreement to Congress. Although this decision was not made public, the Japanese side learned of it from assorted Washington lawyers and Japanese embassy contacts; indeed, the Japanese acquired more information than many American officials had access to. But the information was misinterpreted. The Japanese side believed, wrongly, that the agreement was to be submitted to Congress in mid-March because the U.S. administration appreciated Tokyo's need to settle the issue in advance of its impending deadline for fiscal-year budgeting.[13] In reality, Tokyo's deadlines were of no concern to Washington.

At the end of February, Commerce Secretary Robert Mosbacher met with Bush and Scowcroft at the White House. Mosbacher declared, "George, we have a new administration. We have to get rid of the baggage from the Reagan years. The FSX involves American military technology. As the new president, don't you have to make the decision on this?"[14]

Scowcroft, who had been in the White House during the Gerald Ford years as national security advisor, had an accommodating style and offered an opposing point of view. He argued that the agreement that had been negotiated and signed protected U.S. military technology transfer and that Congress was likely to focus on the production percentage. Mosbacher, however, insisted that trade in U.S. military technology was in a crisis and that now was the time to correct the errors in the FSX agreement. Bush listened to the two men and then said, "Brent, you ought to listen to what Bob is saying."[15]

Expecting Congress to balk at approving the November 1988 agreement and to insist on greater U.S. participation in the project, Secretary of State James Baker wanted to ask Japan to agree to increase the U.S. share of production from 30 to 40 percent. But when Baker met with Foreign Minister Uno, Baker spoke indirectly, rather than directly, and his comments were interpreted positively by the Japanese side. Uno indicated that if the United States was asking for renegotiation of the FSX deal, Japan "can't agree."[16]

When the Japanese eventually learned that the United States was pressing for a 40 percent share of production, they were dismayed. The Bush administration seemed to be demanding a complete revamping of the November 1988 agreement. The Japanese side's point man in the negotiations was Ryozo Kato of the Foreign Ministry, who had substantial experience in Washington and was well liked in diplomatic circles. Kato described the FSX negotiations as "the most unpleasant in his career."

On March 19, 1989, a Sunday, Kato met with Carl Jackson at Kato's home in Bethesda, Maryland. Jackson handed Kato a memo. Looking it over, Kato thought it announced the burial ceremony for the FSX.

Jackson told Kato that Baker wanted to meet with Ambassador Nobuo Matsunaga the following day at the State Department. Kato went to Dulles Airport to meet Matsunaga, where he showed the ambassador the memo in the car. Matsunaga read the memo in silence and then told Kato, "First I have to figure out Baker's true intentions" *(shin-i)*.[17] Kato sent the memo (in great secrecy) to the Foreign Ministry in Tokyo, where three top-level officials set about preparing a response.

Arriving at the State Department, Matsunaga rode the elevator to the seventh floor, where he sat waiting silently outside the Treaties Room portrait gallery. Expecting to see only Baker at the meeting, he was startled to find that Secretary of Defense Dick Cheney was there, along with Mosbacher and Scowcroft. The surprised Matsunaga was surrounded, seated between Mosbacher and Baker on a sofa facing a fireplace. Kato and Bill Clark of the State Department were also in the room.

Matsunaga had met Baker before, for a one-on-one meeting. But this was something else again—four cabinet secretaries at one time. Baker seized the moment for dramatic effect: "We want to talk to you about the FSX agreement. Because of congressional opposition, even if the agreement goes to the floor, it won't be approved. So we think we should 'clarify' the agreement."

Matsunaga wondered what was going on. In Japanese, "clarify" is literally translated as *meikakuka suru*. Was this what the secretary meant? There were other interpretations, which Matsunaga did not offer at the meeting. Did Baker have *minaosu* ("reevaluation") in mind? Or was he suggesting *saikento* ("review")? If either of the latter two meanings was intended, then the two governments would have to renegotiate the agreement. Baker insisted that this was not his intention; rather, he wished to seek clarification of certain points within the framework of the November accord. This was simply a diplomatic nicety, however, for Baker was in fact demanding *minaosu*.[18]

Baker gave Matsunaga a memorandum in which the Americans called for "clarification" on three points: clarification that the U.S. share of production was to be 40 percent; clarification of the scope of the military technology that the United States was to provide to Japan; and clarification of what high technology Japan would provide to the United States.

Just as the presence of the four cabinet secretaries clearly signaled that the Bush administration was unified on the issue, the memo clearly showed that the administration was determined to revise the FSX accord.

The next day, March 21, Bush and Baker both spoke publicly of the need to clarify points in the agreement. "Clarify" was used in part to avoid embarrassing members of the Reagan administration who had negotiated the agreement, and the White House press corps did not appreciate the significance of the use of the term at this point. Its meaning was not lost on the Japanese, however, who understood that they were being asked to make further concessions.

Nishihiro arrived in Washington on March 23 after an urgent summons from Matsunaga. Once in Washington, he traveled up Massachusetts Avenue to the State Department, where he met the same group that had confronted Matsunaga. Nishihiro presented a note from Prime Minister Noburo Takeshita, imploring the United States not to force renegotiation of the FSX accord. Baker just glanced at it and tossed it on the table. His treatment of Nishihiro was icy.

Such a cold response was rare for Baker. Matsunaga later suggested that whenever Baker was inflexible in negotiations with other countries, he was prompted by concern for the real or anticipated reaction from Congress. Because Baker's hands were tied, there was little for the Japanese attending the meeting to do but smile politely. Nishihiro, however, had just arrived in Washington and was not fully abreast of the situation, and he launched into an argument against the three-point memorandum.

In Tokyo, Kichiro Tazawa, the JDA head, held a press conference on March 31, following which he summoned the relevant JDA officials to his office for a stinging rebuke. "Why can't you tell the Americans what you ought to tell them?" Tazawa demanded. "Japan isn't the one who breached the agreement. America is. Why on earth have you allowed yourselves to become so cringing toward the Americans?" As one of the officials recalled, "It was more humiliating than anything I'd experienced in my entire bureaucratic life."[19]

Tazawa's emotional reaction had stemmed from the nationalistic response of the LDP's defense *zoku* ("tribe") to what had happened. On March 29 the top Japanese defense policy groups convened to deal with the crisis. For reasons of secrecy, defense policy Diet members had not been kept informed of details of the negotiations. Incensed by this slight, hard-liners among the senior politicians wanted to return the negotiations to square one. If the U.S. Congress had been informed, they asked, why hadn't the Diet?

The Japanese government was split between hard-liners, such as the JDA, and more flexible groups, such as the Foreign Ministry. MITI's stance had softened somewhat compared to its earlier hard-line position in the negotiations, but, like other ministries, MITI asked itself, "If Japan agreed to 'clarify,' would this be enough? How much more would the U.S. side then demand?"

Negotiations from this point centered on two questions. First, would the Japanese have production responsibility for the engine? Second, how much flight-control source code and data on the fighter's flight patterns would the Japanese get on the F-16? The Japanese side agreed that the United States would have 40 percent of both production and development, but only on condition that on the engine Japan would have over 50 percent.

In Tokyo, Prime Minister Takeshita appointed his deputy chief cabinet secretary, Ichiro Ozawa, to head the negotiations. Ozawa was thereafter at the hub of the negotiating process, conducting a daily airing of views among the Foreign Ministry, MITI, and the JDA and coordinating with Yamamoto, Nishihiro, and the Japanese embassy handling the Washington side of the negotiations. Ambassador Matsunaga's goal in this delicate process was to fathom what Japan could offer that would satisfy the U.S. Congress and Baker.

The answer from Washington was that whereas the Japanese side wanted to retain licensed production in Japan of a U.S. engine, the U.S. side, to maximize its production share, wanted to manufacture the engines in the United States and then ship them to Japan.

In early April, Ozawa visited the Ministry of Foreign Affairs, where he asked for a stiff drink. Whether it was the libation or Ozawa's skill at political wheeling and dealing, the matter was finally resolved, with Ozawa persuading the various Japanese agencies and ministries to accept the need to make concessions. On the basis of that understanding, an agreement was reached on April 28 at the U.S. State Department, with Matsunaga and Kato representing the Japanese. The Japanese made several concessions, agreeing that the U.S.-based companies would receive 40 percent of production, that the source code for aviation control would not be transferred by the United States, and that Japan would give the United States access to the technology it developed for this project. Matsunaga and the Japanese were literally, perhaps, agreeing to "clarify" the earlier agreement; clearly they dared not reject the U.S. demands because of the possibility that to do so would fracture the U.S.-Japan alliance.

Although Japan had bowed to U.S. pressure to "clarify" an agreement that even in its November 1988 incarnation struck most Japanese as overly favorable to the United States, the April 1989 agreement still met with strong U.S. opposition. On May 16, the Senate passed a resolution demanding further specification of the agreement. President Bush vetoed the resolution. In September a powerful group of senators sought to overturn that veto; they failed, by one vote.

Yet American dissatisfaction with the agreement paled in comparison to the response within Japan. The Japanese signed the final agreement

with no enthusiasm and with profound resentment toward their negotiating counterparts. According to military analyst Ryuichi Teshima, the
FSX negotiations were "the bitterest U.S.-Japan negotiations in the postwar era." And the agreement signed in April 1989 was "the most unequal
treaty since the end of the Edo period."[20] Few Japanese would have dis-
agreed with this judgment.

CONCLUSIONS

One cannot understand the FSX negotiations simply by chronicling and
weighing the offers, counteroffers, proposals, and counterproposals that
accompanied the bargaining process. Atmosphere, perceptions, and politics were crucial, penetrating and permeating the process in significant
ways. In the middle years of the 1980s, each side had doubts, suspicions,
and distrust about the other side's motivations, policies, and goals. To
American negotiators, no Japanese proposal could be taken at face value;
every move was part of a carefully conceived master plan conducted by an
evasive, deceptive, and dissembling team of negotiators. Each item on the
FSX bargaining agenda was drenched with subjective meaning, conjuring
up phantoms of Japan's militarist past and the specter of its reemergence,
and reminding Americans of Japan's rising industrial might and the potential threat that posed to the United States.

Likewise, to the Japanese, no American proposal could be taken in good
faith, without probing the motives behind its submission. In Japanese eyes,
U.S. negotiating moves were heavy-handed attempts to keep Japan in a subordinate position. During the negotiations over FSX, Japan sought to escape
this junior role and assert itself. Indeed, one of the chief reasons for undertaking the FSX project in the first place was to demonstrate Japanese independence. As one American analyst of the topic argues, the idea of an
indigenously produced fighter itself was motivated in part by the desire to
"empower Japan within the alliance" and "increase leverage vis-à-vis the
United States in defense technology negotiations."[21] In the event, the
Japanese bid for leverage backfired. Rather than empowering itself, Japan
ultimately underlined its status as the junior partner in the relationship.
Rather than winning a negotiating edge, Japan reprised its accustomed role
as the defensive player in the relationship, repeatedly retreating from its

bargaining positions under heavy U.S. pressure. According to one official in the JDA, "The FSX incident was the opening act in a U.S.-Japan military technology war, and Japan suffered a total defeat. What an utter mess."[22]

However, although the FSX negotiations were unusual in terms of the intensity of ill feeling they generated on both sides, in many other ways they were typical of politicized encounters between Japan and the United States. In this case, as in the negotiations over imports of oranges and rice chronicled in the preceding two chapters, the Japanese revealed themselves to be fundamentally reactive and defensive negotiators. They sought to limit the scope of negotiations and to avoid missteps, and when pushed by the U.S. side they retreated time and again. Whereas U.S. officials were chastised for not pushing hard enough, Japanese negotiators were criticized for not resisting hard enough.[23]

Japan did exert itself in seeking to avoid discussing particular issues or to minimize the scope of the issues that were discussed. For instance, Japan would avoid responding directly to U.S. proposals; make noncommittal responses to U.S. proposals; avoid making explicit numerical commitments and unambiguous statements of policy; delay or postpone decisions; and seek to present the FSX issue as a purely military and defense matter, not one involving trade, technology, or politics.

Japanese tactics had the effect of dragging out the negotiating process, whether or not they were consciously designed to do so. According to Teshima's sources, the Japanese side thought that in time the Americans would back off and that stalling would work to Japan's advantage.[24] But James Auer, who was director for Japanese affairs at the Pentagon from 1979 until 1988, argues that the time factor in these negotiations worked to Japan's disadvantage, giving the U.S. aerospace industry and its congressional allies time to rally opposition to the FSX plan, which in turn led to the United States revising its demands upward.[25]

Making Concessions

The FSX negotiations offer a strikingly clear example of the way Japanese make concessions when dealing with Americans on a high-priority topic in a highly political context. The Japanese side typically would stake out a position, bend when the U.S. side applied heavy (some would say heavy-handed) political pressure, draw a line at a reduced level, retreat once again when confronted by U.S. pressure, take yet another firm stand, then retreat again, and so on. Japan had embarked on the FSX negotiations hoping to assert its independence, but eventually it found itself chiefly concerned with figuring out what could be offered to the United States that would satisfy Secretary of State Baker and the Congress.[26]

Japanese concessions were made incrementally, as the following list shows:

❖ Japan "agrees to consider" the option of joint Japanese-American development of the FSX and "agrees to consider" new U.S. design proposals in contractor meetings (mid-1986).

❖ Japan abandons its proposal for Japanese-led joint manufacture of an entirely new FSX and accepts joint development of the FSX based on an existing American aircraft (June 1987).

❖ Japan agrees to use the F-16 fighter as the basis for the FSX (October 1987).

❖ Japan accepts an MOU (November 1988).

❖ Japan agrees to "clarification" (i.e., renegotiation) of the November 1988 accord, withdrawing its previous refusal to reopen the negotiations (early 1989).

❖ Japan accepts that the United States will do 40 percent of the production of the aircraft, rather than the previously agreed-on 30 percent; that the United States will not reveal the flight-control source code; and that all FSX-related technology developed by Japan will be handed over to the United States (April 1989).

Japan did make efforts to adopt a more positive, active, and aggressive stance, but those efforts tended to be short-lived and ineffective, at least in regard to improving the terms of settlement. Assertive Japanese statements and messages were withdrawn quickly after U.S. resistance, without notching gains for the Japanese side. For example, in mid-1987 Kurihara proposed Japanese-American collaboration on a wholly new FSX, not based on an existing U.S. fighter. Rather than pursuing the proposal aggressively, however, Tokyo immediately dropped it when Armitage and Weinberger rebuffed the idea.[27] Kurihara and Nishihiro both enjoyed reputations as tough negotiators, but the FSX negotiations do not demonstrate that their vaunted toughness accomplished anything.

The Japanese side's strategy was basically to minimize the American share of development and production while maximizing Japanese control over the design, structure, technology, and subsystems of the aircraft. Tokyo's Plan A had been to develop the technology for its own fighter aircraft; having knuckled under to U.S. pressure to accept joint development, Tokyo switched to Plan B, which had much the same objective as its Plan A: Japanese development of critical FSX technologies, but now within the confines of a cooperative program with the United States.[28] Plan B sought the same end as Plan A, but "without exposing the Japanese commitment to the original idea of autonomous development."[29] As an MHI executive viewed it, the American and Japanese conceptions of "joint development" *(kyodo kaihatsu)* were "as different as heaven and earth."[30] The American side wanted Japan to adapt an existing U.S. fighter; the Japanese side wanted to design and produce the aircraft themselves, with as little American involvement as possible. The two sides, to use a Japanese expression, were "lying in the same bed, but dreaming different dreams." Successive concessions left the Japanese side's dream of autonomy in shreds.

(Mis-)Reading the Situation

The bulk of Japanese writing on diplomacy and international relations focuses on understanding what's happening outside Japan, on reading the situation and then adjusting to it. The aim is to understand the environment, not so much in order to manipulate it, as to see what missteps and mistakes to avoid.

In the FSX negotiations, Japan demonstrated an impressive ability to acquire information about the negotiating situation, and in particular about U.S. plans. In March 1989, for example, the Japanese were able, through a variety of channels, to obtain information that the secretive Baker had kept from his own subordinates at the State Department, who were embarrassed to learn about the U.S. plans on FSX from Japanese officials! However, throughout the negotiations, the Japanese proved surprisingly prone to misreading the information they obtained and the signals they received. For instance, Tokyo mistakenly interpreted the Tsutsui mission as having received a green light to proceed with a domestically produced FSX. Tokyo officials and negotiators also misread the Bush administration's decision to submit the FSX agreement to Congress in March 1989 as an indication that the administration was taking into account the Japanese budgetary deadlines, when in fact the decision had nothing to do with sensitivity toward Japanese bureaucratic niceties.

Internal (Dis-)Unity

How unified was the Japanese side during the FSX negotiations? One American analyst contends that the Japanese were in virtual lockstep: "The Japanese side did not suffer from . . . disunity and confusion over goals. Their negotiators represented the key interests within the government committed to indigenous development of a Japanese national fighter. They knew what they wanted and how to get it."[31] This judgment seems highly questionable, however. The Japanese side was *not* unified in its endorsement of a policy for indigenous development of the FSX. And there was nothing close to a national consensus regarding the FSX issue in Japan that would have improved Japan's bargaining position with the United States.[32]

It is true in general that U.S. pressure, by creating resentment in Japan, bolstered Japanese determination to maximize its indigenous R&D capabilities. In the case of FSX, the Technical Research and Development Institute of the JDA, MITI's Aircraft and Ordnance Division, Japan's Air Self-Defense Force, the LDP defense *zoku*, and the Defense Production Committee of Keidanren (Japan's most powerful business organization) all proceeded until 1985 with full consensus and confidence at the working level that the jet would be developed autonomously. When the issue of domestic production became politicized in a bilateral setting in 1986, however, these sections, divisions, and institutes had their policies altered or overturned as their parent organizations moved to protect their broader constituencies and institutional objectives. As Teshima notes, the defense policy politicians were not even kept informed of the details of the negotiations in early 1989. The Japanese government was divided between soft-liners, notably in the Foreign Ministry, and JDA-led hard-liners, with MITI somewhere in between the two camps.[33]

It must not be forgotten that, from the beginning, the coalition for domestic production represented a plurality of interests. There was no monolithic strategy. As the Japanese adage goes, "There is a section but no bureau, a bureau but no ministry, and a ministry but no government." To unify these parochial interests and loyalties requires strong political leadership and skilled bureaucratic management, both of which were in short supply on the Japanese side on FSX. Bureaucratic pluralism created fault lines that would widen and eventually split the coalition as the political and technological opportunity costs mounted.[34] Indeed, FSX was a classic turf battle among MITI, the Foreign Ministry, the JDA , and others over the terms of the MOU.[35]

From 1985, when the FSX project was placed on the Japanese-American negotiating agenda, until protype production began in 1993, the FSX issue concerned, challenged, confused, and confounded successive groups of Japanese and American negotiators and the top political leadership of their respective governments. More than any other bargaining encounter of the period, the wrangling over FSX illustrates how atmospherics can impair the bargaining process and how an impaired process, in turn, can jeopardize chances of an agreement and even shake the foundations of ties between the two countries. In many other ways, however, the FSX case was not at all unusual, and it demonstrates typical Japanese negotiating behavior and tactics.

As in bargaining over agricultural imports, so in negotiating for development of a high-tech fighter plane, the Japanese adopted a fundamentally defensive and reactive posture when dealing with the United States. Given the asymmetries of power between the two nations, it may be doubted if a more aggressive and proactive Japanese stance would have been any more successful in securing Japan's goals. Still, it is instructive that the Japanese side made so few efforts to assert itself or to wrest control of the negotiating agenda and the negotiations themselves from the Americans. Apparently, Japanese negotiators are more comfortable on the back than on the front foot.

4

RENEGOTIATING THE U.S.-JAPAN SECURITY RELATIONSHIP, 1991—96

Ezra F. Vogel and Paul Giarra

From the early 1970s onward, the U.S.-Japan relationship developed a dualistic character. Where matters of trade were concerned, the relationship grew more contentious and acrimonious, degenerating into a series of trade wars that left each side resentful of and frustrated by the other. On security and military issues, relations were perhaps not always harmonious, but they were manageable on the basis of tacitly agreed-on and very different roles for each partner.

The Japanese role was to maintain constitutionally limited and relatively modest air, maritime, and ground Self-Defense Forces; defend itself against direct attacks and "limited and small-scale" invasions; and provide bases and access to facilities and areas in Japan for American forces. The role of the United States was to provide strategic security guarantees and power-projection forces capable of regional and global operations while maintaining significant air, land, and naval forces in Japan.

It was a peculiar relationship. Fundamentally, Japan had long had two opposite worries about the presence of U.S. forces. One was fear of being entangled against its own interests in a war should the United States enter a conflict with China, Russia, or other powers. The second concern was that, at a critical moment, Japan would be abandoned by the United States, which, in accordance with the Nixon Doctrine, was determined never again to be involved in a land war in Asia and was looking to greatly reduce the size of its forces in Asia.

As Japan became richer and the trade imbalance grew, Americans accused Japan of being a free rider. Japan responded by offering to play a larger role in funding support for the American presence (and by the end of the Cold War was paying $5 billion annually) and in furnishing economic aid for developing countries.

93

For many Japanese, the presence of American bases in Japan—the same bases that had been used during the Occupation—seemed to amount to a continued occupation, and they expressed strong opposition at the times of the renewal of the alliance in 1959–60 and in 1969. After Okinawa's reversion to Japan in 1972, Japanese opposition to the Security Treaty gradually came to center on Okinawa. Japanese sympathy for Okinawans and ambivalence toward the security pact led to broader support within Japan for the Okinawan resistance to the presence of American bases on the island.

When the Cold War ended, neither side had a clear consensus about how to refashion the alliance, but groups in both countries recognized the need for change of some kind, including a more explicit assumption of increased responsibility by Japan. Whereas the exigencies of the Cold War had persuaded both countries to do nothing that might undermine their security alliance, with the demise of the Soviet threat political and economic-sector pressure mounted in the United States to redress long-standing trade friction and the asymmetries of bilateral economic relations. The immediate result for the alliance was a period of mutual antipathy and domestic fractiousness that gave both countries pause for thought. Complicating matters further was China, no longer a foil against the Soviet Union. As a rising power whose role was uncertain, China created new uncertainties. The Clinton administration began in 1993 with a focus on economic issues, but crises on the Korean Peninsula and in the Taiwan Strait soon forced renewed attention to defense matters. In 1991, Principal Deputy Assistant Secretary of Defense Carl Ford and others in the Pentagon had begun to wrestle with the question of what the rationale of the U.S.-Japan security relationship was to be after the end of the Cold War. The answer—spelled out in more detail from 1994 to 1996 in what came to be known as the Nye initiative, named after Assistant Secretary of Defense for International Security Affairs Joseph Nye—was that the alliance would reaffirm its fundamental importance to bilateral relations, maintain stability in the Asia-Pacific area, and cooperate in responding to emergencies in the region, particularly on the Korean Peninsula.

The Nye initiative sought to bring bilateral security objectives and military responsibilities and operations into line with the new regional and global environment, emphasizing new responsibilities for Japan, especially close to home. This process eventually involved remarkably close, cordial, and fruitful cooperation, much of it informal, between diplomats, defense officials, and military officers from both sides. As laid out in a memorandum submitted to Nye in the summer of 1994 by Ezra Vogel, the national intelligence officer for Asia, and Paul Giarra, the senior country director for Japan at the Department of Defense, the idea behind the initiative was that plans and agreements would first be worked out at lower levels and then affirmed with some modifications at increasingly higher governmental levels. The process culminated in the Japan-U.S. Joint Declaration on Security Alliance for the Twenty-First Century, signed in April 1996 by President Bill Clinton and Prime Minister Ryutaro Hashimoto, and it led directly to a bilateral review of defense guidelines and Okinawa base issues.

This success owed much to the existence of broad support for U.S.-Japan relationship among key groups on both sides and to the broad-based consultations that followed. In the complex relationships between democratic countries, where various parties play important roles in shaping policy, policymakers can rarely effect significant changes without first securing the involvement and support of a critical mass of influential players in the wider policymaking community. Between 1994 and 1996 an active program of consultation led to common understanding and agreement among such groups in Japan and the United States. When Nye and Vogel left government, however, there was less contact between the full range of players, and progress in implementing the understandings proceeded at a slower pace.

Despite this limited success in implementation, the story of the Nye initiative offers a remarkable contrast to the three cases presented in the preceding chapters of this volume. In place of the difficulties—even animosity—that attended those three protracted and painful negotiations, the defense relationship proceeded relatively smoothly and speedily, with both sides coming together in common purpose to exploit a brief window of opportunity for tangible progress.

In this chapter, we examine the background to this negotiation, describe its course, and explore what it tells us about the ability of Japanese and U.S. officials to adapt their negotiating behavior to pursue new goals, with a broad range of participants, and take advantage of new circumstances. Written by two collaborating participants from the U.S. side, this account gives an inside view of the debates within the U.S. government departments involved, and among the negotiators themselves. Although we tell the story of the negotiation mainly from the American side, we also explore the motives, perspectives, and actions of the Japanese players in this unusually effective bargaining process.

The novelty of the approach taken in the mid-1990s can best be appreciated in the light of the historical context in which it was developed. Accordingly, we begin with a discussion of how the U.S.-Japan security relationship evolved after Word War II, and how security negotiations were conducted during that period.

FROM COLD WAR TO GULF WAR

The U.S.-Japan security alliance was established by the Security Treaty of 1951, which sought to plan for the relationship after the end of Allied occupation the next year. Japan was to provide bases and logistical support for the American military in Japan but was not to develop offensive capacities or nuclear weapons. In return, the United States would extend its nuclear umbrella over Japan and provide security guarantees. These respective responsibilities, further elaborated in the Treaty of Mutual Cooperation and Security of 1960, continued throughout the Cold War.

Japan, however, was reluctant to take on further responsibilities. The Japanese paradigm of strict avoidance of any entangling defense cooperation with the United States, beyond providing bases for U.S. forces and turning a blind eye to what those forces did and where they operated during peacetime, severely limited the range and outcomes of defense discussions. While security relations during the Cold War were relatively manageable after 1969, with relations between American officials and their Japanese counterparts usually friendly and cooperative, nevertheless they were starkly limited in scope, with the Japanese consistently resistant to American attempts to broaden the relationship.

This resistance was inspired by what Japanese officials usually described for American colleagues as "severe domestic political restraints." Within Japan there was widespread distrust of centralized government power, an attitude represented perennially within the Japanese government by the Cabinet Legal Bureau, which took it upon itself to block more explicit security cooperation through consistently restrictive policy interpretations of Japanese laws and actions. Japanese politicians and bureaucrats were generally unwilling and usually unable to overcome these constraints. They were also restrained by their constituents' and their own political misgivings about a more active role for Japan in military matters, fearing the bogeyman of resurgent militarism in a more independent Japan.

It was accepted Japanese practice to avoid arrangements and agreements with the United States that would lead to any loss of national prerogatives, to entanglements with American regional or global actions, or to complications for Japan's regional diplomacy. Japan preferred to conclude ambiguous agreements or no agreements rather than utter an explicit "No" to American requests. This reflexive Japanese resistance was a way by which Tokyo leveled the playing field with Washington in the bilateral security relationship and protected national equities in what appeared to be a straightforward exchange of bases in return for security guarantees.

The Liberal Democratic Party, which governed Japan for almost forty years, from 1956 until 1993, made it consistently and abundantly clear during the Cold War that the domestic accommodation with American security interests could be pushed only so far. Direct Japanese political or military support would not be possible except in the case of a direct attack on Japanese territory. The availability of Japanese bases for wartime operations other than in the strict defense of Japanese territory was dependent on the purposely vague concept of "prior consultation," which required that in the event of a crisis the United States would have to ask the Japanese cabinet for authority to use Japanese bases for offensive strikes against, say, the Soviet Union or North Korea. Despite its fundamental irrelevance for American plans requiring specificity, and despite the potential danger for American commanders bereft of Japanese support, this ambiguous and enigmatic arrangement, an adaptation to Japanese political realities, was never seriously questioned during the Cold War.

Operational integration between U.S. and Japanese forces, which had always been minimal, generally diminished as the Self-Defense Forces assumed responsibility for defending Japanese territory, taking the place of, rather than working with, American units. At the same time, Japanese contributions, such as indirect material support provided during the Vietnam War, were pushed to the limit, but more explicit agreements were strictly controlled. The few quiet agreements that established tangible operational cooperation, such as intelligence sharing and antisubmarine patrols in the Sea of Japan, were not made known to the Japanese public and often were not even widely known within the government of Japan, thereby severely constraining their more widespread utility.

Virtually every notion of cooperation beyond the established accommodation that the Treaty of Mutual Cooperation and Security represented— bases in exchange for security—was simply off the table. The emphasis remained squarely on the defense of Japan (Article 5 of the Security Treaty); little attention was given to regional security responsibilities (laid out in Article 6). Sympathetic relays of American diplomats and military officers were reminded to good effect that Japanese generals and prime ministers who even alluded to more direct bilateral cooperation were routinely and summarily sacked. There was no question that the character of the alliance—designed to administer bases but not to fight—was not going to change until external circumstances changed.

The late 1980s and early 1990s finally brought change. The end of the Cold War in effect placed Japan back in play as a geopolitical entity after more than forty-five years of stasis. With the demise of the Soviet Union, the U.S.-Japan alliance lost its common purpose, and Japan lost a nearby enemy for which it had cultivated a universal domestic antipathy for almost a century. In its relationship with the Russians, Japan never experienced the ambivalence that characterized its history with its more problematic Asian neighbors, especially the Koreans and the Chinese. The new post–Cold War strategic circumstances were going to require very different Japanese political and military approaches, and new and revised relationships with the United States and regional neighbors.

Just as the Cold War was drawing to a close, the purpose and character of the U.S.-Japan security relationship was thrown into yet greater question by the war to evict Iraq from Kuwait. Japan found itself constitutionally and politically restrained from giving direct support to the American-led coalition in the Persian Gulf. Under the existing political and constitutional circumstances, dispatch of the Self-Defense Forces to participate in wartime operations or in a combat support role was out of the question. Japanese merchant seamen refused to transport military and other cargoes in support of the coalition in Japanese-flag vessels. The popular response in Japan to the invasion of Kuwait was ambivalent and did not support overt Japanese involvement. The best that the alliance could do was to deploy American forces stationed in Japan to the Persian Gulf and muster a $14 billion Japanese financial contribution to the Gulf Coalition Council. This Japanese response was so little (in terms of personnel) and so late that when Kuwait took out an advertisement in a U.S. newspaper to thank nations that offered assistance, Japan was not included in the official list, even though Japan's financial contribution was greater than any other nation's. For the alliance, this failure was a shock that galvanized a push for change in Japan in both Washington and Tokyo.

AN UNEASY, UNCERTAIN RELATIONSHIP

With the end of the war in the Persian Gulf in 1991, the U.S.-Japan security relationship was in a quandary. Bilateral relations were tense, with uncertainty over security roles exacerbating a sharpened debate over trade and economic issues. The end of the Cold War accentuated bilateral differences, especially the economic asymmetries, which had been purposely downplayed in order to preserve a united front against the Soviet Union. Like defense, trade was an area where long years of negotiations had failed to open Japan fully and where disagreements persisted.

Once Japanese industry had begun to produce more sophisticated products in the 1970s and Japanese exports were posing stiff competition to American industry, the U.S. business community exerted great pressure to limit Japanese exports and, later, to open Japanese markets. The highest level of American officials in Washington and in the embassy in Tokyo generally considered these trade issues less important than the security issues and tried to prevent U.S. trade officials from putting the security relationship at risk. But by the late 1980s, when the Japanese economy threatened to overtake the U.S. economy in such high-tech areas as semiconductors and in such basic industries as automobiles, trade discussions became increasingly tense. With the end of the Cold War in 1989, and the subsequent collapse of the Soviet Union, there was no longer any clear rationale for constraining U.S. trade and economic pressure. The focus of the bilateral U.S.-Japan relationship began to shift markedly, at the explicit expense of the security relationship. Conflict over trade heightened in the early 1990s, and would grow worse—peaking in the first two years of the Clinton administration—before it got better.

From the end of the Cold War, Japan was under severe pressure to take a larger security role. The example of Americans shedding blood in the Persian Gulf War while Japanese merchant seaman refused to carry military cargoes haunted alliance managers in Washington. They knew that a war on the Korean Peninsula would be much bloodier and that much closer to home for Japan, but that without substantial change Tokyo's response might be just as vacillating and noncommittal or worse, incapable of providing organized domestic support.

In Japan, too, there were those who wanted Japan to play a more active role for their own, nationalistic, purposes, and who adroitly leveraged American pressure. By this time, significant consideration had been given in Japan to an enhanced Japanese military role. Ozawa Ichiro, an influential Diet leader, made the case for learning from the failure to commit Japanese personnel during the Gulf War. The Japanese military buildup in the 1980s, the result of close coordination between President Reagan and Prime Minister Nakasone in response to the Soviet invasion of Afghanistan, had given impetus to considerable speculative planning in Japan. For instance, by 1988 the Japanese Maritime Self-Defense Force (JMSDF) had developed plans to expand the Self-Defense Fleet considerably, with additional, and larger, flotillas centered on new, small aircraft carriers as flagships. However, neither the domestic political situation in Japan nor the strategic circumstances before 1991 were sufficient to support such significant change.

The earliest publicly distinct indication of Japan's changing approach to external security after the end of the Cold War was the dispatch in 1991— generally perceived as too little, too late, but in both context and reality a giant step forward—of JMSDF minesweepers to the Persian Gulf to assist with postwar mine clearance. Admiral Makoto Sakuma, then chief of staff of the JMSDF, had prepared elements of its minesweeping force for deployment to the Persian Gulf in 1990. It was not until after the war was over, and Sakuma had been elevated to the post of chairman of the Joint Staff Council, that the JMSDF was able to deploy, but its mine-clearing operations in the Gulf proved significant internationally and revolutionary domestically. This action, without precedent in post-Occupation Japan and taken virtually without political debate, let alone constitutional or legislative authority, set the precedent not only for subsequent peacekeeping deployments but also for the legislative security transformation still under way today. Sakuma's action meant that no longer was *everything* off the table in alliance security negotiations.[1]

In 1992, shortly after the precedent-setting deployment to the Persian Gulf, Japanese legislators passed the International Peace Cooperation Law, which permitted for the first time tentative and limited Self-Defense Force participation in peacekeeping operations. In its first test, Tokyo dispatched ground and air Self-Defense Force troops in 1992 on two consecutive, six-month, battalion-sized deployments to provide engineering support to the United Nations Transitional Authority in Cambodia.

Notwithstanding these signs of an increasing Japanese readiness to assume a more active international role, the Japanese government was far from united on the question of whether the country should accede to U.S. demands that it shoulder a larger alliance military burden. For example, the Diet froze many critical (by U.S. standards) peacekeeping functions when it passed the peacekeeping bill in 1992, thereby consigning the Self-Defense Forces to a strictly limited mission profile that amounted to the provision of simple humanitarian assistance.[2]

Insufficient unity within the Japanese government on this question was a reminder that Japan rarely if ever makes a move without first establishing its own internal consensus. Opportunities for clarifying and forcing that consensus would come later. However, despite the lack of clarity concerning what should come next, it was clear in the early 1990s that if Tokyo failed to respond effectively to a new emergency closer to home— and an emergency in Korea was a distinct possibility by 1993—the outcome would be disastrous for the alliance. American political support would evaporate, and the demand to "stop defending Japan" would most likely cause the end of the alliance.

In Washington, as in Tokyo, uncertainty over the future of the alliance prevailed, not least because of endemic bureaucratic competition and the lack of domestic political consensus. Just as the Japan Defense Agency (JDA) and the Ministry of Foreign Affairs (MOFA) competed directly for domestic influence, so did the U.S. State Department with the Department of Defense. Indeed, U.S. efforts were further hampered by the

perennial east-west competition between Washington agencies—the
Pentagon and the State Department, in particular—and the American
embassy in Tokyo and United States Forces Japan Headquarters, which
as often as not strove to use their proximity to and frequent contact with
the Japanese government to gain control of political-military policy and
alliance management issues.

Seldom was there a critical mass of concurrence on the American side.
When all American parties were represented at the U.S. interagency table
at which U.S. policy was meant to be fashioned, the process was rigid and
competitive and provided little opportunity for the emergence of internal
consensus, let alone progress with Japanese counterparts. Conversely,
when individual agencies, departments, and military services were in discussions with the Japanese, they had no credible authority for reaching
explicit agreements, even though negotiating progress as often as not
depended on deal making by individuals.

With State, Defense, and military interests competing with one another
and with those of the White House, Commerce, Treasury, and other
departments, the U.S. national decision-making process was effectively
hobbled. It was impossible to bring any substantive program of change to
the table. And in any case, had there been a coherent American proposal for
concerted alliance action, or more than rhetorical Japanese support for
American military operations, it would have been met with instinctive
resistance from many powerful interests on the Japanese side. In such cases,
Japanese negotiators would effectively retreat behind their pleas of legislative, policy, and political obstacles, often quoting weak political leadership
as their primary impediment. Essentially, during 1991–92 the two national
systems were out of synch internally and with each other.

More fundamentally, there was no clear view on either side of what the
alliance should become, were change ever to become feasible. Those in a
position to effect change presented no clarifying vision for the future;
those who had such views were incapable of delivering their own governments to the negotiating table.

Perhaps the nearest that the two sides came to trying to reconcep-
tualize their relationship at this stage was a process launched by Principal
Deputy Assistant Secretary of Defense Carl Ford. Ford was responsible
for launching a series of Defense Department Asia-Pacific white papers,

first known as the East Asian Strategy Initiative (EASI), and then later and more familiarly as the East Asia Strategy Report (EASR). The first EASI report ("A Strategic Framework for the Asian Pacific Rim," issued in April 1990) and its 1991 successor were reports to Congress. They anticipated congressional interest in Pacific theater troop-strength adjustments as a result of the end of the Cold War and were designed to preserve Department of Defense leadership of the strategic planning process. These reports were part of a larger interagency effort to incrementally reduce the size of U.S. forces in the Asia-Pacific theater.

As early as the spring of 1991, Ford had begun quiet discussions regarding possible future concepts for an invigorated alliance. He did so in part by meeting discreetly, and often separately, with his JDA and MOFA counterparts. These discussions concentrated on the concept of enhanced Japanese rear-area support for American operations from and around Japan, and on a Japanese emphasis on military peacekeeping operations as a first step toward assuming greater responsibility for external security. This was an explicit attempt to redress the imbalance between Japan's considerable but carefully circumscribed responsibility for the defense of Japan and Tokyo's reluctance to become involved in or take responsibility for regional security, most notably on the Korean Peninsula.

It was clear, however, that both Ford and his interlocutors had limited authority and little room for maneuver, and that these discussions were more of a philosophical first step than substantive negotiations. In the early 1990s there was not the broad support, within either the U.S. or the Japanese government, for a reconceptualization of the U.S.-Japan relationship. Like other discussions at the time that passed for negotiations, this preamble to later progress led by Ford was limited and low-key, and it lacked any chance of yielding agreements in the near future. Even so, these discussions marked the start of a process of negotiation that began to change the terms of the security relationship—a process that was to culminate more than six years later with the approval of new Defense Guidelines.

A STYLIZED AND STERILE NEGOTIATING FORMAT

For the most part, these and other Japanese-American negotiations in the first few years after the end of the Cold War followed long-established formats. Highly stylized bilateral policy discussions, led by Washington and Tokyo, included very infrequent meetings of the Security Consultative Committee (SCC). The SCC brought the U.S. Defense and State Departments together with Japan's Foreign Ministry and the Japan Defense Agency for defense policy talks at the secretarial/ministerial level. Derivatives of the SCC met more frequently: the Security Sub-Committee (SSC), which met at the level of assistant secretary/director general; and the Mini-Security Sub-Committee (mini-SSC), which met at the level of deputy assistant secretary/deputy director general. They operated in distant parallel with the workmanlike but rigid in-country Joint Committee process that administered the Status of Forces Agreement governing the bilateral agreements on bases and the presence of American forces in Japan. The SCC process dealt with broad policy issues that almost never changed. In contrast, the Joint Committee dealt, at a much lower level, with much more tangible issues and the reality of domestic politics and constraining legal interpretations that directly affected U.S. forces in Japan.

In 1990, the composition of the SCC was changed. Where previously the U.S. ambassador in Tokyo and the commander of the U.S. Pacific Command had met with the Japanese foreign minister and the chief of the JDA, henceforth the secretaries of state and defense would represent the United States. The new arrangement was known as the "2+2" and its high-level cast represented the promise of broader support and enhanced symmetry. However, the first full 2+2 meeting did not occur until September 1995 (and then it took place only on the margins of an ongoing UN General Assembly meeting) and the neuralgia of the formatted meetings did not ease.

In terms of process, individual conversations between policy and political officials embellished the formatted plenary process in a less constrained environment, as often as not on the margins of the more routinely scheduled SSC and frequent mini-SSC meetings. National delegations traveled frequently between Tokyo and Washington, from the secretarial level on down (although the secretary of state almost never went to Tokyo), for discussions that were sometimes purely diplomatic or military in character, sometimes mixed, and often included American military representation from the Joint Staff, Pacific Command, and U.S. Forces Japan. Like the

American delegations, the Japanese delegations were bloated by the requirement to include almost every agency and command with an interest in the talks, and they typically included MOFA's North American Affairs Bureau, JDA's Defense Policy Bureau, and uniformed Self-Defense officers of the Joint Staff Office. For reasons of bureaucratic infighting on the Japanese side, the Japanese delegations did not include representatives from MOFA's Asian Affairs Bureau or the JDA Equipment Bureau. The Ministry of International Trade and Industry (MITI) and the Ministry of Finance also were excluded, thereby constraining U.S. participation as well.

Routine contacts between defense officials and diplomats and the Washington and Tokyo embassies played an important role in the process, as did individual forays by both senior-level and working-level officials, but their discussions were often less than authoritative unless enhanced by extraordinary circumstances or unusually clear discrete authority. At every level progress was routinely circumscribed by the lack of either consensus or authority.

When bureaucratically influential officials were in place and engaged, it was much easier at least to *imagine* that progress was possible. One notable Japanese example was Seiki Nishihiro, the first person to rise within the JDA's ranks to the top bureaucratic position of administrative vice minister (usually, the top officials at JDA were transplanted from the Ministry of Finance, MITI, or the National Police Agency). Dynamic and thoughtful, Nishihiro inspired and mentored a generation of JDA officials and was personally responsible for recruitment and personnel management that raised JDA's stature, abilities, and morale. His influence is strongly felt to this day. Another champion for a more balanced bilateral relationship and the assumption by Japan of greater security responsibilities was Shigeru Hatakeyama, JDA's Defense Policy Bureau director general and subsequently its administrative vice minister. (Nishihiro and Hatakeyama were both heavy smokers and died early of cancer.)

Given the institutional constraints Hatakeyama faced, his especially close personal relationship with Carl Ford was extraordinarily effective and productive, as was Nishihiro's relationship with Richard Armitage, who had served as U.S. assistant secretary of defense for international security affairs from 1983 until 1989. Their partnership was emblematic of how the bilateral alliance management system had come to depend for

progress on side meetings and personal initiatives and individual agreements rather than concerted, top-down negotiations that confronted
common issues and examined alliance responses.

It was with Ford that Hatakeyama first envisioned the outlines of change
for the alliance, and he energized the JDA to replace its ethic of devising
increasingly contrived ways to say "No" to concepts of greater Japanese
defense responsibility with one of looking for imaginative and new ways to
say "Yes." However, he was a bureaucrat who needed cover and authority
from elected politicians to be truly effective in the Japanese system, and that
sponsorship was largely lacking.

Individually and in sum, these various activities generated more heat
than light. Ford and Hatakeyama had begun to explore a new, more balanced, alliance; nevertheless, despite the growing awareness that the changing global and regional context called for some kind of redefinition of the
U.S.-Japan security relationship, neither side had a clear idea of how to
proceed.

Nor did either side have a sufficient political rationale for forcing change
in the security relationship. On the contrary, Japan's body politic and public generally opposed both closer, encumbering ties with the United States
and a more active international role for Japan, and Japan's powerful bureaucracies reflected this view. Furthermore, Japan's ministries and agencies
were locked in competition that stifled initiatives, and the country's top
leadership produced a succession of weak prime ministers and cabinets.

On the U.S. side, officials had to contend with the fact that the ability of
the State and Defense Departments to set the U.S. agenda with Japan had
been sharply diminished by the sudden boost in the influence accorded
to commercial and economic interests. Not until the security situation on
the Korean Peninsula worsened shortly after the U.S. election in 1992 did
the two sides begin to recognize the need for action to redefine the bilateral alliance.

NEW APPROACHES

Carl Ford's successor late in the administration of George Bush, William
Pendley, developed these early discussions into broader and more proactive sessions, starting in the summer of 1992 at the National Defense

University in Washington. However, Japanese participants made it clear from the outset that they had no authority to proceed beyond tentative discussions that would carry no definitive weight in Tokyo, and the discussions were tightly restricted.

Participants in this tentative but pivotal process on the U.S. side included the Office of the Secretary of Defense (OSD), USCINCPAC (the U.S. Commander in Chief, Pacific, headquartered at Camp Smith, Hawaii), U.S. Forces Japan (headquartered at Yokota Air Base), and the American embassy in Tokyo. Participants on the Japanese side included MOFA, the JDA, and the Joint Staff Office. (Typical of American ill-discipline, throughout this period the Joint Staff conducted a parallel, competing series of discussions with the Self-Defense Forces that was deliberately concealed from other U.S. alliance managers. Although the Joint Staff effort also pushed the Japanese to accept more responsibility for defense, it tried to move Japan much further than U.S. strategic interests, policy consensus, or Japanese politics would allow.)

With several interruptions, these quiet discussions proceeded at the working level through 1995. Led by the United States, they used American-designed war-gaming extensively as a new means of defining and clarifying both sides' requirements and expectations. These seminar war games were conducted in such a way as to avoid commitment by the Japanese participants, who clearly were under orders to preserve plausible deniability for the Japanese government.

The scenarios played out in the games focused on the Korean Peninsula, and they introduced and outlined the concept of Japanese rear-area support for American operations. The end result was a working list, based on the principle of gradual expansion of Japanese responsibilities, of just over a dozen mission areas in which Japan could provide direct military support for American operations or rear-area logistical support for U.S. forces; this list enabled the Japanese to acquire an exceptionally detailed conceptual understanding of American requirements. Although agreement was not in sight, misunderstandings and opacity in a very sensitive and delicate exploration of future possibilities had been greatly reduced.

Nonpapers were another tool used extensively, especially from 1993 onward, in which unofficial "draft" documents were exchanged at the desk officer level in order to define positions and introduce new ideas.

Given their plausible deniability, nonpapers were a convenient, hard-to-misconstrue, and risk-free way to organize and embellish the exploratory discourse that was becoming more active between the United States and Japan. Relatively simple to prepare bureaucratically, and often drafted collegially by colleagues from both governments, nonpapers typically represented working-level consensus and set the stage for subsequent supporting bureaucratic and political-level decision making.

Variations on the theme included the public diplomacy series of Department of Defense Pacific defense white papers chartered by Carl Ford (see pp. 102–103) and, in its most highly developed form, the National Defense University's Institute for National Strategic Studies McNair Paper 31, *Redefining the U.S.-Japan Alliance: Tokyo's National Defense Program*, which laid out American concerns regarding emerging Japanese defense policies and strategies (see below, p. 115).

A New Administration in Washington

With the inauguration of the Clinton administration in January 1993, the determination of senior U.S. officials to push for quantitative Japanese targets for the import of U.S. manufactured products and the determination of the Japanese to resist made for tense bilateral relations. With the Cold War over, the new American administration was philosophically determined not to allow national security concerns to interfere with the U.S. emphasis on bilateral trade issues. In 1993 the Clinton administration established the National Economic Council to push Japan on setting numerical targets for American imports. Clyde Prestowitz, a Commerce Department official in the Bush administration under Secretary of Commerce Malcolm Baldridge, had made a very strong case to the public after he left government service that during the Cold War America's efforts to get a satisfactory balance of trade with Japan had not been effective because trade issues were always subordinated to security issues. With the end of the Cold War, he asserted, it was no longer necessary to sacrifice trade to security.

U.S. negotiators, including within the Defense Department, began not only to push harder at the expense of the security relationship but also to use the security relationship for the benefit of U.S. trade policies, most notably in the FSX fighter aircraft work-share negotiations and in theater missile defense discussions. Seeing this, many on the Japanese side grew increasingly dubious about the level and longevity of U.S. commitment to Japan's security, especially now that their common enemy, the Soviet Union, had disappeared. On the U.S. side there were also considerable concerns about the relationship, especially regarding the credibility of Japanese support, the difficulties of sustaining so asymmetrical an alliance, uncertainties about how to respond to a rising China, and the contradictions inherent in an economically competitive but militarily cooperative alliance.

There ensued a period of intense but ill-defined and unfocused U.S. interagency debate over Japan policy in Washington. Several attempts to craft a unified policy concept that balanced trade, politics, and security failed. The debate bogged down when no clear interagency or even single departmental notion of trade and political priorities and requirements emerged. The traditional outlines of the security alliance persevered almost by default.

As detailed in the previous chapter, negotiations over the FSX project during the Bush administration generated considerable ill feeling on both sides. Likewise, the issue of theater missile defense (TMD) inspired considerable ambivalence. Americans and Japanese had been discussing missile defense since the late 1980s, in the shadow of President Reagan's "Star Wars" Strategic Defense Initiative. American and Japanese companies had formed two industry teams and participated in a study on missile defense in the Western Pacific. Japanese government participation per se was explicitly precluded, however, although the government was kept informed of progress and briefed on the outcome. There were few tangible results beyond the paper study.

By the first months of 1993, the issue of theater rather than strategic missile defense had begun to gain considerable momentum, and the two governments had formed the bilateral U.S.-Japan TMD Working Group. However, other discussions regarding new concepts for alliance cooperation and responsibility sharing were seriously deflected by the emergence—from within the Office of the Secretary of Defense—of the concept of "Technology for Technology" (TFT), according to which U.S. defense systems would continue to be available to Japan only if Tokyo shared advanced defense-related technologies with the United States. This new tack startled Tokyo. The United States was interested in a more equitable relationship, or at least in extracting some advantages from a presumably rich and capable store of Japanese technology. For Japan, however, national equities and its ability to deal relatively equally with a far more powerful ally were at stake. In essence, this was an American assault not only on certain Japanese commercial interests but also on Japan's strategic core values of technological and political independence and economic prowess—a notion that had more psychological and political relevance than substance, given the few areas in which Japan can compete or contribute scientific and R&D wherewithal.

This precipitous Pentagon attempt failed, not least because after the initial overture its proponents failed to determine what specific Japanese technologies might be useful or desirable. TFT also suffered from never having been coordinated, or fully vetted, even within the Department of Defense, and it ignored the consensus-oriented realities of decision making in Japan and those ingrained, cautious, and incremental practices of the alliance regarding new initiatives. Given the American discord, it was easy for Tokyo to stonewall.

From the beginning Tokyo resisted reflexively both general American overtures for more cooperation and specific initiatives such as TFT. The standoff highlighted the differing national negotiating approaches: the United States treated technology as a commodity; Japan treated technology as a strategic resource. Japanese technology was seen as the fuel of its economy, and it was perceived in Tokyo if not in Washington as the main armament in Japan's increasingly explicit and neomercantilist economic competition with the United States.

THE NORTH KOREAN NUCLEAR CRISIS

In the meantime, the North Korean nuclear crisis of 1993–94 emerged to coincide with the gridlock of Japan policy in the U.S. interagency decision-making process. Korea became an urgent issue because North Korea was threatening to continue to produce fissionable materials that could be used to build a small arsenal of nuclear weapons. The United States had long pressured South Korea not to develop nuclear weapons, and the development of nuclear weapons by North Korea, then defined as a rogue state, was deeply destabilizing. The United States put a great deal of pressure on North Korea to stop the production of fissionable materials. North Korea threatened conflict, the reality of a North Korean nuclear capacity loomed, and tensions arose from the danger that war might break out on the Korean Peninsula.

The possible consequences of a crisis on the Korean Peninsula for the U.S.-Japan alliance had engaged the Pentagon's alliance managers for some time, especially after the Gulf War. Even superficial comparisons with the Gulf War made it clear that not only Japan but also American planners were woefully unprepared for another Korean conflict. The Gulf War had also revealed Japan's predisposition to sit out rather than to engage politically or militarily. As we have noted (see above, p. 107), North Korea had already become the strategic planning case for deducing structural changes that would have to take place in the bilateral security relationship. This planning case accepted that Japanese financial contributions alone, as provided to the Gulf Coalition Council, would not suffice in an Asia-Pacific crisis that challenged the alliance directly, especially one in which the United States was likely to sustain substantial casualties.

A conflict with North Korea would mean massive combat requirements: Japan would become a base for American logistics and almost certainly for operations. Presumably this would require that Japan play a role analogous to that performed by Saudi Arabia during Operations Desert Shield and Desert Storm. A detailed, carefully conceived, practical bilateral agreement would have to be negotiated in advance and physical preparations made for both logistics and operational support.

However, not only did no such plan exist; there was not even the context for one. Over many decades Japanese negotiators had carefully delimited the parameters of discussions and cooperation on security. American plans existed for the defense of South Korea. Japan and the United States both had their own national plans for the defense of Japan. However, no *bilateral* plans had been drawn up, even for the defense of Japan. The bilateral U.S.-Japan alliance was totally unprepared for effective U.S.-Japan action against North Korea, beyond what the United States could do unilaterally and short of combat operations from Japan. Unrealistic American and Japanese planning presumptions remained in place: that all combat would occur on the Korean Peninsula, and all logistical support would be provided by American units stationed in Korea and operating elsewhere in the region.

At the height of the crisis, U.S.-Japan discussions that had begun at the National Defense University in 1992 were put on hold in order not to impinge on sensitive discussions between Washington and Seoul. The U.S.-Japan alliance reverted to its Cold War character during this period. Quiet overtures to Tokyo ensured that Japan would support the United States politically and, if the time came, would permit combat operations from Japan, but without any operational or logistics specifics identified or pledged, or planning envisioned, let alone conducted. Washington finally recognized that this cryptic and grudging approach was not only no way to run an alliance but also downright dangerous. This realization became a major motivating factor in the subsequent U.S. emphasis on alliance security measures and the concerted push for rationalization and change.

In the end an international framework was agreed on under which North Korea would cease production of nuclear weapons and the Korean Energy Development Organization (KEDO)—to be directed by representatives from the governments of the United States, South Korea, and Japan—would provide diesel fuel and later a light-water nuclear reactor for generating electrical power in North Korea that would not use materials that could be employed for weapons production.

As the danger of the North Korean nuclear crisis began to recede, the United States and Japan were able to refocus on the future of their alliance. Those involved knew that 1995 would be a testing year: it marked the fiftieth anniversary of the end of World War II and thus would challenge both sides to concentrate on the future rather than the past; it was also the year in which the agreement under which Japan paid some of the costs of U.S. forces in Japan was due for renewal. In addition, Japan would revise its National Defense Program Outline (NDPO), its twenty-year defense industrial plan.

By early 1994 U.S. security officials were also becoming concerned that the continuation of base agreements, particularly in Okinawa, was in doubt. The U.S. military was frustrated that many specific negotiations were being held up—operational planning discussions; negotiations to simplify contracting and payment procedures for the exchange of military goods and services; and new pressure from Japan for changes to the Status of Forces Agreement—making it difficult to formulate bilateral plans for the defense of Japan. Many of these specific agreements were difficult to achieve without a broader common understanding of where the U.S.-Japan security relationship was heading.

A NEW OUTLOOK IN TOKYO

Since 1990, Japan had been receiving briefings on drafts of Department of Defense Asia-Pacific white papers. From 1992, Japanese reactions were taken into account in finalizing the texts. This proved an unusually strong and tangible basis for mutual understanding and helped to ensure some continuity in the alliance as the strategic environment evolved. Nevertheless, from Tokyo's perspective, it seemed clear that the United States was devaluing its alliance with Japan. Even so, Japanese defense planners felt that Japan was occupying an increasingly marginal place in U.S. strategic calculations. The Department of Defense's 1990 EASI report had, after all, announced a three-stage reduction of U.S. forces in Asia.

Tokyo's desire to ascertain exactly what place it was likely to occupy in the Clinton administration's planning helps explain why, in February 1993, Tokyo dispatched Foreign Minister Michio Watanabe to Washington, D.C. During his trip he met President Clinton and Secretary of State Warren Christopher and was the first foreign visitor to meet with the new administration's secretary of defense, Les Aspin. Signaling that there was now at least tentative high-ranking political support for efforts to reevaluate the alliance, Watanabe agreed to permit low-level discussions of new alliance modalities, thus authorizing negotiations past and future.

The timing and the subsequent course of events were ironic. With Watanabe's visit, the Foreign Ministry had granted explicit authority for tentative discussions regarding the future of the bilateral security relationship just prior to the fall of the LDP government in 1993. With this authority, quiet discussions between Tokyo and Washington continued after the LDP was replaced by a series of governments led by "civilian internationalists," who were even more reluctant to make military commitments than their LDP predecessors. The first such government was formed by Morihiro Hosokawa's Japan New Party; the next was led by Tsutomae Hata; this was followed by an LDP–Japan Socialist Party coalition led by Prime Minister Tomiichi Murayama. These new leaders had no desire to strengthen and rationalize the U.S.-Japan security relationship and lacked a domestic consensus to draft bilateral military plans.

This shift did not go unnoticed in Washington, of course. As a practical matter, however, alliance managers had to wait for incontrovertible evidence of a more distant Japan before they could make a compelling case for increased attention to bilateral security issues and the future of the alliance.

Nevertheless, for the first time, the working-level discussions that had begun in the summer of 1992 could proceed in the hope that they might have some practical influence on the security relationship. Role-playing and seminar gaming continued to be used to explore the boundaries of potential alliance cooperation, specifically in the case of a crisis in Korea. However, these bilateral sessions never ventured beyond the North Korea scenario to investigate other regional challenges such as that posed by the standoff between Taiwan and the People's Republic of China. The terms of the discussion were set very narrowly, and the alliance never took the chance to proceed further, conceptually or tangibly.

In early 1994, a number of Japanese officials expressed their frustrations to their U.S. counterparts. They were uncertain about continuing U.S. commitments, and yet they had to draw up Japan's new National Defense Program Outline (NDPO), which would establish Japanese defense priorities for the next twenty years, and they were about to begin their new planning cycle for the next five-year Mid-Term Defense Program.

A NEW ATTITUDE IN WASHINGTON

The Higuchi Commission Report, a first draft of Japan's high-profile, civilian-led governmental group advising on the preparation of the NDPO, was issued in the spring of 1994. This public report and the entire Japanese process of defense review were viewed in Washington as an explicit trial balloon in advance of the publication of the NDPO itself in 1995. As a wake-up call it succeeded admirably. The Higuchi Report reflected the effect in Japan of the perceived lack of a clear U.S. commitment. It talked of the necessity for Japan to have a hedging strategy; since U.S. actions were uncertain, Japan should prepare for the option of doing more on its own and depend on the United Nations and other multilateral institutions for security. Continued Japanese reliance on the Security Treaty with the United States was relegated to a lower priority.

American attention was galvanized not just by the Higuchi Report, but by the frequent concern expressed by Japanese officials at all levels that they could not move ahead with their defense planning without a much clearer understanding of what the United States was doing. It was plain that without assurances from the United States and a clear sense of over-all direction, the relationship between the United States and Japan would continue to drift, if not diverge. The result was likely to be a more inde-pendent Japanese security policy, with the prospect of engendering reac-tions throughout Asia—particularly among the Chinese—that might easily lead to an arms race and spiraling tensions.

These fears were discussed at length between U.S. and Japanese officials at the working level in Washington. The frankness of these discussions was unusual and reflected the growing tendency for new approaches in bilateral negotiations to spread from the bottom up. To an unprecedented extent, junior American and Japanese officials were coming together to sketch out policy approaches that would be taken up as whole cloth by the more reg-ularized consultative negotiating process. It was made clear by the Amer-ican side in these discussions that the Higuchi Commission Report was out of step with notions of a strong alliance, and that renewed emphasis on bilateral alliance solutions was necessary.

As one direct result of this concern, Patrick Cronin, director of studies at the Institute of National Strategic Studies of the National Defense Uni-versity (NDU), published an internal study he had written for the Office of the Secretary of Defense with Michael Green, an OSD consultant from the Institute for Defense Analysis (IDA). Their study became NDU's McNair Paper 31, *Redefining the U.S.-Japan Alliance: Tokyo's National Defense Program.* "All things being equal," the authors observed, "the U.S.-Japan alliance is Japan's first choice, but there is a growing question [in Japan] about whether it should be the *only* choice."[3] Cronin and Green concluded:

> Decisive action is now necessary to redefine the alliance. Lingering uncer-tainties about the Korean Peninsula demand the establishment of clear rules for operational cooperation—including acquisition and cross-servicing

agreements (ACSA), base access, and host nation support. Future bilateral cooperation in theater missile defense will depend on agreement on joint operational requirements reached in the near term. The commitment of the Japan Defense Agency (JDA) to the development of redundant (possibly destabilizing) systems for long-range airlift, maritime support, and perhaps satellite surveillance will be determined in large measure by forward-looking U.S. policies to improve interoperability and intelligence sharing for Japan's peacekeeping operation (PKO) missions. Indeed, U.S. actions and initiatives to redefine the overall security partnership with Japan must be carefully considered during this time of comprehensive reassessment in Japan.[4]

This conscious, public revelation of what were essentially the themes of the American negotiating position helped shape discussions for the next several years.

The American side noted with some satisfaction that when the NDPO itself was published in 1995, the primary importance of the alliance to Japan's security was mentioned no fewer than thirteen times. This was the proximate result of very direct, sometimes blunt, discussions conducted in the spirit of McNair Paper 31 and as part of the subsequent Nye initiative.

ORIGINS OF THE NYE INITIATIVE

By early 1994 it had become clear to Assistant Secretary of Defense for International Security Affairs Charles Freeman just how uncomfortable Japanese leaders and bureaucrats were with the state of the alliance. In the context of the North Korean nuclear crisis and direct expressions of Japanese unease, Freeman saw that the alliance was not only ill prepared for major conflict in Korea but also unable to cope with any significant degree of stress. The alliance was drifting, with no one at the helm. He made his concerns known to Under Secretary of Defense for Policy Walter Slocombe and to Secretary of Defense William Perry. Plans to redress the situation began to be laid out at the working level in the Defense Department.

At the time of this renewed interest and concern, Joseph Nye was head of the National Intelligence Council and Ezra Vogel was national intelligence officer for East Asia. (The two men were faculty colleagues on leave from Harvard University.) Vogel called a number of meetings in the first half of 1994 at the National Intelligence Council to analyze the problems with the U.S.-Japan relationship. Among the participants were Commander Paul Giarra, the senior country director for Japan; his deputy, Lieutenant Colonel Robin Sakoda; Patrick Cronin; Michael Green; David Asher, a young academic working at IDA; Jim Delaney, former CIA station chief in Seoul and Tokyo and now semiretired, working at IDA; and Andrew Saidel of the CIA, who like Mike Green had served as an aide to a member of the Japanese Diet.

By late summer of 1994, Secretary Perry agreed with Freeman and Slocombe that Slocombe should kick off an intensified round of discussions with the Japanese leadership. In October 1994 Slocombe traveled to Tokyo and prepared the way for Nye, who was about to take over in the Pentagon from Freeman.

When Nye arrived at the Pentagon in late autumn, he immediately made it clear that Japan would be his highest priority. Vogel had made the point to Nye that nothing would do more to reassure the Japanese and to stabilize the U.S.-Japan relationship than an overall broad examination of the issues by interested parties on both sides. Confronted with many concrete issues such as base arrangements, technology sharing, joint planning for emergencies, the Japanese found it difficult to deal with concrete issues without a clear sense of where the relationship was headed. Furthermore, such an examination, searching for general agreements and crystallizing specific points of view, would give both sides a much greater assurance that their alliance was stable than if it were managed by a small group of people who simply signed an agreement without such a broad basis.

Vogel and Giarra presented Nye with a memorandum that suggested holding a thorough discussion of bilateral security issues between various levels of the U.S. and Japanese governments. They recommended continuing the effort to give Tokyo a clear understanding of the logic of what the United States was doing in the East Asia Strategy Initiative process of deliberate and phased force reductions hinging on improvements in the relationship with North Korea. They also made the case for expressing to the Japanese a renewed commitment, which had emanated from the Defense Department and spread throughout the U.S. government, for a security relationship adapted to the new circumstances of the post–Cold War era.

This renewed emphasis on closer security relations was made possible because, by this time, the contentious interagency process of the previous year had exhausted itself. Bureaucratically, State Department officials at the Japan desk within the East Asia Bureau were under pressure to emphasize economic issues at the expense of security issues. Competition between the East Asia Bureau and the Economic Affairs Bureau weakened the influence of regional affairs at the State Department.

The Defense Department, now bolstered by Secretary Perry's sponsorship of the Nye initiative, was able to step up to the plate to fill the gap and take the lead. Perry's leadership was a major, fleeting achievement that enabled the success of much of what followed.

Officials concerned with East Asian security at the State Department and the White House were consulted and approved of the plan that was drawn up, to be spearheaded by the Defense Department. Nye took charge of the initiative that was named after him, with an intense and personal interest. The daily details were under the direction of his Japan desk officer, Giarra. Vogel took responsibility for keeping on track the combined Defense–State Department working group that was formed to structure and execute the one-year Nye initiative, and he worked with numerous officials in various parts of the Japanese government. At the State Department, Tom Hubbard, principal deputy assistant to Assistant Secretary for East Asia Winston Lord, kept abreast of developments and lent his support.

Throughout the course of the initiative, Nye kept Secretary of Defense Perry informed of plans and progress. Perry became the initiative's most senior sponsor and Cabinet spokesman, and it was to him that the White House delegated authority for the initiative. Stanley Roth, in charge of Asian security at the White House, was kept informed and supported the initiative, but he was busy with other projects and did not play a central role. No other high-level U.S. officials were deeply concerned or involved, and neither Secretary of State Warren Christopher nor National Security Advisor Tony Lake ever engaged to any noticeable degree. Nor did any members of Congress play significant roles. Security issues, in fact, were not a major issue in Congress at the time, and while members of Congress such as the Democrat Representative Lee Hamilton and Republicans Senator Richard Lugar and Representative

Doug Beureuter were kept informed and were generally supportive of these efforts, they were not centrally involved in the initiative. Since the issue was not politicized, the American press, like Congress, took little interest in the initiative.

At the U.S. embassy in Tokyo, with Fritz Mondale as ambassador, Rust Deming as deputy chief of mission, and David Shear as the political-military officer, there was a very effective team capable of working well with Japan and the appropriate officials in Washington. Mondale was very sensitive to the political mood and, at a time of extremely rapid transition between prime ministers, kept in touch with the key political leaders in Japan and was able to respond quickly. Deming combined a broad perspective with intimate knowledge from many years of involvement in security issues. Shear was very effective in coordinating with MOFA and the JDA.

In Washington, Nye, Vogel, and others made sure that they gave updates about the initiative to the small community of influential former officials from both parties who were well informed about security issues with Japan—and whose views were commonly solicited by high-ranking political officials in the White House and Congress. This group included such people as Michael Armacost (former ambassador to Japan), Richard Armitage (former assistant secretary of defense and special ambassador), James Kelly (former NSC staffer and deputy assistant secretary of defense for East Asia), Douglas Paal (former National Security Council senior director for Asia), James Auer (former director of the Japan desk at the Pentagon), William Clark (former assistant secretary of state for East Asia), and Bill Breer (former deputy chief of mission in Tokyo).

On the basis of this broad-ranging support from the various quarters of the U.S. policymaking community, mid-level U.S. officials pressed ahead with their Japanese counterparts in planning and developing the effort. A bottom-up approach was by no means unprecedented, although it is much more typical on the Japanese side, where lower-level officials generate ideas and higher-level officials arrange the consensus to support implementation of that idea. What had been missing on the U.S. side was the breadth of discussions and a champion. At different levels, Perry and Nye filled these requirements perfectly.

THE EAST ASIAN CONTEXT

In Washington there was by late 1994 a general and growing acceptance of the working group's consensus on the need for this alliance-building effort to include broad-based discussions on a framework for the post–Cold War era. The essential logic was that in the period following the Cold War, joint U.S.-Japanese planning would not focus on enemies, as it had when the potential threat from the Soviet Union shaped the alliance's posture. President Bush's secretary of defense, Dick Cheney, had first introduced this notion in a speech delivered at the Tokyo Press Club in late 1991. The conceptual emphasis on partnership with Japan rather than on peril from China constrained the character, relevance, and extent of U.S.-Japan negotiations consistently and significantly.

The United States wanted both a stable framework for security in the East Asia region and a dependable base for U.S. troops and supplies. American bases in Japan would continue to enable the United States to respond to emergencies as they arose, including emergencies as far away as the Persian Gulf.

In concept, Japan and the United States acting explicitly together would deal directly with emergencies in "areas surrounding Japan," such as the potential nuclear threat from North Korea. Japan's alliance role would evolve and expand modestly, but in a way designed to strengthen confidence in the alliance, to promote mutual cooperation, and to maintain stability in the region.

Underlying this American approach was the conviction that it was important first to firm up the alliance with Japan, and then for Japan and the United States both to begin working in a more positive way to strengthen their relationships with Beijing. To begin security discussions with the People's Republic of China (PRC) while the U.S.-Japan alliance was in disarray was likely to create great uncertainties between Washington and Tokyo and misunderstandings with Beijing.

U.S. discussions with Japan were limited generally to strictly bilateral alliance issues. Insofar as China did come up in discussions, the Americans and Japanese agreed that they should deal with the PRC in a constructive manner as a future partner and should engage it in broad-ranging discussions once their security alliance had been put on a firm footing. Even so, throughout the Nye initiative little attention was given at higher levels to addressing Chinese concerns about the future shape of the U.S.-Japan relationship. To reduce the chance that China would over-react to U.S.-Japan security discussions, Vogel met occasionally with a high official in the Chinese embassy in Washington to keep him informed of the progress of the discussions. More effort, however, should have been devoted to relaying the same information to a much wider range of PRC officials, especially at the higher levels in Beijing. Such an effort might have prevented the very negative reaction from China to the U.S.-Japan initiative that eventually ensued.

THE WORK PLAN

With Nye established at the Pentagon by late October 1994, the working group that had formed around the idea that the alliance was adrift and needed serious attention began its work in earnest. Fortunately, that summer a U.S.-Japan agreement had been reached that would open the door to more Japanese imports of auto parts from the United States. This averted the possibility that White House officials, determined that Japan first give ground on trade issues, would oppose the security negotiations. Unconstrained by trade considerations, Vogel and Giarra drew up an eighteen-month agenda that took advantage of the calendar and was built around two primary action-forcing events.

The first action-forcing event was the anticipated first-ever full meeting of the 2+2 SCC, scheduled for September 1995 in New York, on the margins of the UN General Assembly meetings there. According to the work plan, when the ministers met in September 1995 they would approve a number of agreements, the details of which were to be worked out in the interim at lower levels. These agreements included a renewal of the 1990 Host Nation Support/Special Measure Agreement by which Japan supported (to the tune of $5 billion annually) the costs of U.S. forces' facilities and nonsalary expenses such as rent and taxes.

The second action-forcing event was the proposed security summit, set tentatively for November 1995 in Tokyo, just after the Osaka Asia-Pacific Economic Cooperation (APEC) summit. The security summit was to be the ultimate driver, at which the two heads of government would confirm the agreements reached at the ministerial and lower levels. Most important, they would sign a security declaration that would outline a new alliance relationship, based on principles relevant to the post–Cold War world. Vogel's and Giarra's job at lower levels was to develop a consensus that would then be passed on to higher levels.

Other important goals laid out in the work plan were achieving a breakthrough agreement on the long-standing but by now dormant Acquisition and Cross-Servicing Agreement; and incorporating into a broad-ranging security declaration a number of initiatives such as a proposed review of the Guidelines for Defense Cooperation for the first time since 1978, which would establish the new respective roles and missions of the alliance partners. (In light of its subsequent importance, it was ironic that the subject of the Defense Guidelines review did not receive significant emphasis when the work plan was first drawn up or in the Security Declaration. It was not until early 1996 that the potential of the Defense Guidelines review to reshape the alliance was fully appreciated.)

In late December 1994, the State Department signed off on the work plan for the coming year drawn up by the Pentagon, and it was transmitted by the Pentagon to the Japanese embassy in Washington on Christmas Eve. By very early 1995, the government of Japan had agreed to this timetable, and one could begin to imagine eventual agreement along the lines laid out in the working-level discussions.

The prospects for progress were encouraging, not least because there now existed on the Japanese side, as on the U.S. side, support for the Nye initiative from a broad array of key groups, including MOFA, the JDA, politicians and influential former officials in Tokyo, and the Japanese embassy in Washington.

At the Japanese embassy, key participants in the alliance review effort were now in place, permitting a bilateral working group to form in Washington that was highly efficient and was given unprecedented latitude to conduct direct negotiations, rather than having to wait for the frequent but constrained meetings of senior officials that characterized the consultative process of the alliance. This desk officer—and first secretary—level group was closely tied to the American Country Team at the U.S. embassy and military commands in Tokyo, and to key high-ranking, influential bureaucratic sponsors in MOFA and the JDA. From this point forward, arrangements and agreements crafted by the bilateral working-level group were routinely approved at higher-level meetings.

In the past, MOFA bureaucrats had dominated the Japanese side of the alliance. As the Nye initiative progressed, all the high officials in MOFA, including the vice minister, councilors, and director generals, were kept informed and played a broadly supportive role, though the direct discussions were conducted by lower-level officials. By 1995 the JDA, and in particular a number of young officials within that agency, began to play a more assertive role. The top ranks of the JDA had generally been staffed by officials from other ministries; the JDA did not have a large group of senior officials familiar with broad aspects of international policy and strategy, which had been generally left to officials at MOFA. During the course of the Nye initiative, JDA officials Shigeru Hatakeyama and Masahiro Akiyama were very supportive. A key liaison role was played by a young Self-Defense Agency official, Nobushige Takamizawa, who was at the National Defense University in Washington as an exchange student during 1993–94. Despite his student status, he was fully engaged in policy negotiations. He had more flexibility than his embassy counterparts and reported directly to the vice minister of the JDA. Senior JDA officials worked to position their juniors to take part in broad-ranging discussions in informal groups, not least because they felt that this experience would strengthen the ability of the JDA to deal with broad international security issues in the future rather than leave strategic issues to MOFA.

When preliminary discussions began in the summer of 1994, Japanese bureaucrats specifically requested that the discussions not involve their political leaders. This request was prompted in part by the fact that the relationship between the bureaucracies and politicians in Japan had changed with the defeat of the LDP in 1993. A close, relatively efficient, mutually rewarding, and predictable working relationship had grown up between the bureaucrats in MOFA and the JDA and the LDP politicians in power since 1955. With the fall of the LDP, bureaucrats suddenly had to work with a variety of parties. The bureaucrats were particularly concerned because the coalition governments that took over beginning in 1993 when the LDP lost its majority were very unstable—indeed, there were five prime ministers within the first year and a half of the Clinton administration. MOFA in particular feared that if politicians became involved, much debate and confusion would ensue, greatly complicating the work of reaching a common understanding. The bureaucrats preferred to work with American counterparts and then present the politicians with a fait accompli and hope that the politicians would see little choice but to agree.

The U.S. side, however, aware that Japanese political leaders would have to be involved in the end, feared that if those leaders were not informed during the discussions and were suddenly asked later to affirm an agreement reached entirely by bureaucrats, they might refuse to go along. The U.S. side therefore decided that it was important to bring Japanese politicians into the discussions from the very beginning. After coordinating with Japanese officials in Washington, Vogel visited Tokyo where he met—quietly and privately—with a number of key political figures. He had lengthy, one-on-one discussions in Japanese with members of two groups. One group was composed of the former prime ministers Nakasone, Miyazawa, and Takeshita, who all still had considerable influence in politics. Vogel had known each of them personally prior to coming into the government in 1993, and these personal relationships served as the basis for an easy exchange of views. This group made it clear that they supported the broad U.S.-Japan security relationship and the efforts that were being made to stabilize it. The second group of Japanese politicians was the defense *zoku* ("tribe"). In Japanese politics there are numerous such tribes, each composed of readily identifiable officials from various parties who are concerned with a particular sectoral issue. The U.S. embassy in Tokyo maintained broad contacts with the members of the defense *zoku*, and Vogel visited each of them individually to inform them of the conduct of the initiative. These politicians approved of the overall purpose of the ongoing negotiations and agreed that the discussions between Japanese and American bureaucrats should continue.

Vogel and Nye also kept in touch with a group of Japanese former officials and intellectuals concerned with defense issues. Men such as Hisahiko Okazaki (a former ambassador to Thailand and Saudi Arabia and once chief of MOFA's planning staff), Seiki Nishihiro (former vice minister of the Defense Agency), Masahiro Nishihara (professor and later president of the National Defense Academy), Seizaburo Sato (formerly professor at the University of Tokyo and head of the secretariat of advisers to Prime Ministers Ohira and Nakasone), and Admiral Sakuma were kept informed of progress. Vogel occasionally met with them, and Nye presented his views to them on a crucial visit to Japan, where he talked with various officials in MOFA.

THE IMPORTANCE OF INFORMAL DISCUSSIONS

After Japan failed to respond to the U.S. request for a strong show of support in the Persian Gulf War, the bilateral collegiality that had prevailed through much of the Cold War was weakened. With the launch of the Nye initiative, however, informal discussions between Japanese and U.S. officials once again became the norm, as often as not outside regular channels, first at the working level and eventually reaching to the ministerial level. The two sides began talking once again. Japanese bureaucrats were very receptive to U.S. suggestions for less formal meetings.

Several influential Japanese junior defense officials were in Washington at the time. Each year a JDA official is sent to the U.S. National Defense University (NDU); Takamizawa was at NDU at the time, and he was considered unusually able and had direct contact with the vice minister, the senior official at the JDA. These postings were peripheral to the Washington embassy and were designed to allow the officials to engage in quiet discussions with their American counterparts, discussions that would generate neither press attention nor unease among a Japanese public that was still reluctant to forge a closer relationship with the United States.

The Pentagon and State Department Japan desks and their Japanese counterparts were exceptionally busy from early 1993 onward, especially during late 1994 and throughout 1995. Vogel occasionally met with Ambassador Takakazu Kuriyama and Minister Hashimoto (a cousin of Ryutaro Hashimoto, who would later become prime minister) to keep them abreast of progress. The key contact, however, was Yutaka Iimura, head of the embassy's political section. He had been at Harvard the previous year, where he had come to know Vogel well, and they met frequently during 1994 to discuss plans for the initiative. Iimura involved two very active political-military first secretaries, MOFA official Masafumi Ishii and JDA-detailed Satoshi Maeda, allowing them frequent and unfettered discussions with their Defense and State Department counterparts. Discussions typically included a succession of Japanese defense attachés, but it was no secret that Takamizawa had more flexibility in his activities than did they.

Participants on both sides in early 1993 set up a discussion group (a *benkyokai*, or "study group"), a bilateral forum for informal discussions on U.S. and Japan security issues. Establishing a *benkyokai* is a traditional Japanese approach to improving understanding and forging a consensus among those individuals working together on a common issue. It was utilized to good effect in the bilateral security relationship in both Washington and Tokyo.

This *benkyokai* was especially consequential. It survived the departure of Takamizawa in June 1995 and of Ishii in January 1996, coming to an end only after the departure of Maeda in June 1997. Takamizawa in particular played a key role on his return to Tokyo in drafting the Defense Guidelines. The study group included both Japanese and U.S. officials at middle and lower levels who represented key ministries and departments, as well as participants from Washington-area think tanks. Patrick Cronin and Michael Green played substantive and socializing roles in formatting and steering the group's deliberations, as well as in providing NDU and IDA venues for informal discussions. Giarra and Vogel were both regular participants.

This approach provided for excellent camaraderie and free discussion in a very relaxed atmosphere. It also permitted blunt talk. It was in these discussions that American dissatisfaction with the Higuchi Report was first expressed, putting the Japanese government on notice regarding American intentions and establishing the outlines of negotiations that set the stage and the agenda for the Nye initiative.

By early 1995 discussions had proceeded very much as planned. If anything, discussion was more broad ranging and cooperation more extensive than had been expected. Discussions touched on broad strategic issues and political concerns but also concentrated on specific security issues such as Japanese support for U.S. bases and rear-area operational and logistical support. The informal working-level talks were complemented and paralleled by more formal, much more discreet, and more technical defense discussions that spelled out American requirements and assessed Japan's ability to respond to new roles and missions.

A Clear Sign of U.S. Commitment

In February 1995, the increasingly positive atmosphere in which security negotiations were being conducted was both reflected in and enhanced by the publication and wide distribution of the first in Nye's series of regional white papers, *United States Security Strategy for the East Asia–Pacific Region.* Written by Nye's Office of International Security Affairs, the report drew on the progress to date in the U.S.-Japan security dialogue. The Japanese participants in these discussions were given an advance copy of the draft report, and their informal responses were accommodated in the report's final version. Sharing the draft with the Japanese was a significant move: Tokyo had been briefed in advance of early EASI and EASR white papers, but asking for Tokyo's input was a new departure. It reflected the U.S. side's desire to build Japan's confidence in the U.S. desire to collaborate, and it was intended to contribute to a shared overall understanding of the situation rather than to tell the Japanese how to write their NPDO. It was this report that contained Nye's famous observation capturing the value and intention of America's commitment: "Security is like oxygen: you do not tend to notice it until you begin to lose it. The American security presence has helped provide this 'oxygen' for East Asian development."

The white paper announced that the United States was still committed to maintaining a level of approximately 100,000 troops in Asia—the number that the Defense Department's "Bottom-Up Review" of October 1993 had deemed necessary to enable the United States to meet its commitments in East Asia. Some American commentators, most of them senior military officers, criticized the 100,000 figure as being too rigid, even though the report clearly stated that this was only an estimate, to be adjusted as technology and regional circumstances required. In fact, critics and supporters read what they wanted into the declaration of intent. Nevertheless, Tokyo took the declaration seriously. The report's main achievement was to strengthen confidence in a continuing U.S. commitment to meet its defense responsibilities in the region.

The 100,000 number came to represent a clear public benchmark, for better or for worse, that Tokyo had to consider in its own political calculations. It also had the effect of bounding internal debate on the U.S. side, establishing the limit of movement in case of dissension in the face of

attempted false economies or attempts at retrenchment, and establishing
that, in effect, there would be no withdrawal from Okinawa. Despite early
and consistent flouting of the requirement by U.S. commanders, the standard gave American negotiators something to point to in their discussions
with Japanese interlocutors as a standard of U.S. commitment.

The Japanese side was receptive to American overtures for clarifying
the security relationship—perhaps more receptive than the Americans
had expected. Within Japan an increasing number of officials realized that
Japan had lost international support as a result of its low level of cooperation during the Gulf War and that Japan's failure to cooperate fully with
the United States in the event of an emergency in Korea would seriously
strain the U.S.-Japan relationship. Japan's own aspirations to play a more
active international role, in the form of Japanese participation in peacekeeping and humanitarian relief operations, were also boosting Japan's
receptivity to U.S. ideas.

The prolonged tension over North Korea's nuclear program and missile developments was having a cumulative effect on Japanese thinking
about its security. Truculent Chinese behavior was also having an effect
on thinking in Tokyo. Even Japan's Socialists, in government (as part of a
coalition) for the first time ever, had by this time accepted the legitimacy
of the security alliance with the United States.

"BEST-LAID PLANS"

The work plan's schedule for progress was affected by external events. Two
crises in particular disrupted negotiations. The first of these was the Taiwan
Strait crisis of 1995–96, which arose when the Taiwanese president, Lee
Teng-hui, paid a "private" visit to a reunion at his alma mater, Cornell
University, in June 1995. This visit to the United States marked a bold, sym-
bolic step toward ending Taiwan's decade and a half of official international
isolation. Lee's repeated use of the terminology "Republic of China on Tai-
wan" in public statements was taken by Beijing as a challenge to its own
"One China" formulation, which envisaged the eventual reunification of
Taiwan and mainland China under Beijing's direction. In response, the
People's Republic of China conducted tests of six missiles from July 21 to
26 in an area only sixty kilometers north of Taiwan's Pengchiayu Island.

The tests came amid a flurry of PRC invective denouncing Lee Teng-hui's visit. The missiles were all MTCR-class: four short-range and two intermediate-range. All were modern, mobile, and nuclear-capable (although unarmed). At the same time, Beijing mobilized forces in coastal Fujian Province and moved a number of Jian-8 aircraft to the coast. The result was predictable: the stock market and the local currency in Taiwan fell precipitously.[5] China staged further missile demonstrations in 1996.

From Japan's perspective, the PRC's actions were alarming. Since the American military withdrawal from the Philippines, China had become increasingly assertive and aggressive in the South China Sea, disputing unsettled territorial claims with its Southeast Asian neighbors. By 1995, the sovereignty of Japan's Senkaku Islands (known in Chinese as the Diaoyu Islands) had become an issue with Beijing, forcing Tokyo to reappraise its long-term relationship with China. This was a crucial time for the bilateral alliance. Nowhere in the Mutual Security Treaty did it say that American security guarantees were limited to Russian or North Korean threats. Tokyo was distressed that Washington did not immediately support Japan in the Senkaku Islands dispute. It was left to the U.S. deputy assistant secretary of defense, in a stumbling, tardy effort to save face, to recall publicly American security guarantees to protect Japanese territory. Neither Beijing nor Tokyo was much impressed.

The second crisis was more directly relevant to the ongoing U.S.-Japan discussions. In early September 1995 an Okinawan schoolgirl was raped by three U.S. servicemen. The news was a political bombshell that shocked both sides of the Pacific and engendered varying responses from those with stakes in the alliance. The Japanese public was outraged. Okinawa's antimilitary and anti-American groups sought to capitalize on the prolonged press attention given to the case and to the future of the overall security relationship. Ambassador Mondale in Tokyo and Secretary Perry in Washington were quick to denounce the rape and to cooperate with Japan in dealing with the issues. The Japanese government and political leadership were largely (and, to some Americans, disturbingly) silent when it came to expressions of support for the fundamental importance and continued relevance of the bilateral alliance. This was especially relevant when the overall security relationship began to be called into question by the Japanese press.

CONSEQUENCES OF THE 1995 OKINAWA CRISIS

The Okinawa rape crisis had two specific effects on the diplomatic discussions under way. First, it complicated and slowed progress toward the agreements and preparations for the planned 2+2 talks later that month and for the security summit scheduled for November. At the same time, it galvanized the attention of U.S. officials, especially those senior members less directly involved but ultimately responsible for substantive progress and for the eventual outcome of the Nye initiative.

Kurt Campbell had taken over as deputy assistant secretary of defense for East Asian and Pacific affairs in May 1995, and by September he was directly responsible for the initiative. He responded dramatically and forcefully to the Okinawan crisis, having concluded that the initial slate of proposals to be included in the security summit agreements was necessary but no longer sufficient. Together with Perry, Nye, Mondale, and Deming, Campbell immediately launched negotiations that led to discussions regarding one clause of the U.S.-Japan Status of Forces Agreement (SOFA), which dated from 1951 and had last been revised in 1960. With both sides energized, new SOFA arrangements were negotiated at the working level that would allow for the early, preindictment transfer to Japanese custody of members of the American armed forces in Japan who are suspected of committing heinous crimes. Not for the first time, the hardest part of the negotiating routine was overcoming internal American resistance. When such resistance from the U.S. military services was overruled, the Japanese side accepted their gains with equanimity, and agreement to this revision of the SOFA was concluded with unprecedented speed, by late October. The episode illustrated how a politically sensitive, cohesive American team could respond sufficiently quickly and forcefully that even volatile, highly emotional issues in Japan could be dealt with in a manner that did not upset the overall U.S.-Japan relationship.

In addition, Campbell settled on the idea of a significant gesture regarding Okinawa bases and introduced what became the Special Action Committee on Okinawa (SACO), essentially a mechanism to return Futenma Marine Corps Base—which occupied a large area of land in a heavily populated area of Okinawa—in exchange for a new facility elsewhere on Okinawa.[6]

The possibility of the return of Futenma energized Japanese political support for the more general agreements being struck in preparation for the forthcoming security summit: Japan would take some responsibility for external security and provide tangible rear-area support to U.S forces and operations; would directly acknowledge the importance of Korean stability to Japanese security; would renew the agreement to continue Host Nation Support payments of $5 billion a year; would ease restrictions on the exchange of defense goods and services; and would agree to a review of the Defense Guidelines.

What had begun as an agreement in principle on how to transform the alliance to better respond to regional security requirements and bring Japanese contributions more in line with American expectations became a horse trade, motivated by the politically and psychologically satisfying prospect of balancing concessions. Japan could more easily acquiesce to American requests for enhanced rear-area support for American military operations if the United States would consolidate U.S. bases on Okinawa and return the Futenma air base.

THE TOKYO SECURITY SUMMIT

One further unplanned disruption was still to come. The U.S. working group was literally en route to Japan in preparation for the scheduled November 1995 security summit, security declaration in hand, when it learned that the president could not leave Washington because of a budget crisis with the U.S. Congress. Although the vice president attended the APEC summit in Osaka in his place, the security summit that was to have taken place immediately thereafter in Tokyo was postponed until the following April.

By the time of the April 1996 security summit, the security declaration was a more explicit, detailed, and far-reaching document than it would have been had it been signed the previous November. In the interim, a new Japanese prime minister had been installed, one who was determined to see Japan play a more active role in its own defense and in the alliance.

Elected in January 1996, Prime Minister Ryutaro Hashimoto led the LDP back to power in national elections and provided very strong, conservative leadership on the Japanese side. Hashimoto, a defense hawk, made his first priority the "nationalization" of Japan's approach to bilateral security negotiations—that is, he sought a more explicit articulation of Japanese national interests and a less passive negotiating role. He ordered that a phrase reiterating Japan's determination to forswear war as a sovereign right—a phrase that had been included by Foreign Ministry negotiators during the tenure of the Socialist prime minister Murayama and that reflected adherence to Article 9 of the Japanese Constitution—be removed from the text of the declaration.

Hashimoto also encouraged a more aggressive and proactive attitude among MOFA officials, most notably the deputy director general of the North American Affairs Bureau, Hitoshi Tanaka, who had been seasoned by personal experience of a decade of contentious trade negotiations. These officials worked hard to secure internal Japanese support for changes in the security relationship with the United States, and they were active in proposing changes to the Americans. They also pushed back against American efforts to extract Japanese concessions.

On April 17, as rescheduled, President Clinton joined Prime Minister Hashimoto for a summit meeting in Tokyo. The highlight of their meeting was the signing of the Japan-U.S. Joint Declaration on Security Alliance for the Twenty-First Century (reproduced in the appendix to this chapter). The Joint Declaration reiterated the fundamental principles governing the security relationship and pledged continuing mutual support, with what promised to be a new Japanese activism. It reasserted the importance of the alliance to regional stability and security, and it committed Japan to security policies with a significantly more pronounced external orientation than before. Japan would no longer implicitly limit its external security efforts to consciously constrained peacekeeping operations: for the first time Japan explicitly recognized that the security and stability of the Korean Peninsula was a vital national interest. (China and Taiwan were not mentioned, and Tokyo made it clear in a publicly conducted internal debate among the leaders of the LDP in the aftermath of the Tokyo summit that neither issue was ready for discussion.)

In addition, after Washington had applied considerable late pressure on both U.S. and Japanese negotiators, the Acquisition and Cross-Servicing Agreement, which had been stalled for eight years, was concluded and signed on April 16, the day before the summit.

The security summit was greeted with jubilation by both sides and by the press. The Joint Declaration was a clear statement of alliance intent and resolve unprecedented since the 1960 revision of the Security Treaty. Furthermore, the sense had grown, and was reflected in public comments and media commentary, that Japan as a nation was on the verge of significant geostrategic change and about to assume a more proportionate share of responsibility for national, regional, and alliance security. Indeed, the White House described the Joint Declaration as the single most important and successful foreign policy achievement of the administration to that time. It represented a successful culmination of the joint U.S.-Japan security initiative of 1994–95.

CONCLUSIONS

Gauging Success

Over the short term, the Nye initiative was undoubtedly a success. Between 1994 and 1996 real progress was made in strengthening the bilateral security relationship after a period of uncertainty and drift. Unlike the heated and acrimonious bilateral economic negotiations, these security discussions were generally cordial and productive. Formal negotiating processes, productive personal relationships, unusually close collaboration, bureaucratic acquiescence, broad support from key groups, and a few champions on both sides who sponsored the initiative combined with external events to facilitate a common understanding of the need to reformulate the alliance and to work together to overcome the political obstacles.

The goodwill, common understanding, and momentum that developed between 1994 and 1996 did not, and probably could not, last. Ironically, given the White House's glowing description of the Tokyo summit, immediately after signing the Joint Declaration the White House turned its attention away from Japan and toward redressing the worsening relationship with China. Joe Nye left the Pentagon in December 1995. The initial agreements reached at the April 1996 summit left many specifics still to be negotiated, including the review of the Defense Guidelines, the implementation of the Joint Declaration's security framework, and the promised return of the Futenma air base in exchange for another facility somewhere on Okinawa. Subsequent negotiations on the details of these and other issues became more difficult and very much localized. Futenma's future, for example, has still not been resolved, because Tokyo must treat base issues as local concerns first, rather than sharing the American perspective of bases as strategic alliance and regional security issues.

Moreover, to this day Japanese actions, policies, and legislation have not been calibrated to meet U.S. military requirements for the defense of Japan and for operations within the region. To be sure, there has been considerable progress in Japanese security legislation and force structure, developments that have accelerated since the attacks of September 11, 2001. However, these changes have less to do with alliance building and the enhancement of U.S. forces operating in, around, and from Japan than with Japan's own nation building and defense normalization. For instance, bringing Japan to bear in the defense of South Korea—a key objective of the Nye initiative—still presents technical, military, and political uncertainties that have not been fully resolved. Even more challenging would be defending Taiwan against an attack by the PRC, a task that would certainly require access to bases in Japan and explicit Japanese political, material, and military support. Long-standing unresolved alliance political issues regarding China and Taiwan would make an immediate coordinated response almost impossible.

As the century drew to a close, the rise of China created new issues. While the growing power of the PRC and Beijing's truculence played a large part in prompting Japan to strengthen its alliance with the United States, Japanese concerns about China also hold Japan back from forging closer ties with the United States. Washington and Tokyo have not had full discussions on the question of whether China might pose a potential threat to their alliance. Japan—apprehensive of Chinese ambitions in the South China Sea and made uncomfortably aware during President Clinton's visit to China in 1998 that he was then more intent on building ties with Beijing than on strengthening the alliance with Tokyo—continues to hedge its bets vis-à-vis the alliance. Some in Tokyo regarded alliance negotiations, the subsequent Defense Guidelines discussions, and the anticipated American military retrenchment on Okinawa as reasons to increase Japan's military power (by expanding the gathering of intelligence, being more willing to send forces abroad to take part in peacekeeping operations, and so forth).

Despite continued Japanese reluctance to clarify and specify the particulars of its support for the alliance (and new security legislation now moving through the Diet may resolve some of this ambiguity), American defense expectations for Japan are higher than they have ever been. Pressure from the United States for significant new Japanese military contributions remains unabated, with enhanced Japanese capabilities seen not only as a complement to U.S. forces in the region and beyond but also as a way to resolve enduring and glaring asymmetries in the bilateral alliance. Japan's deployment of JMSDF destroyers and oilers to the Indian Ocean in support of U.S. Navy operations in the ongoing "war on terrorism" is one sign of its changing international profile and its readiness to change its security policy in order to play a different role abroad. These developments are both a portent of greater future cooperation between Japan and the United States and a sign of an increasingly independent Japan, ready to play a more active international role, militarily as well as economically.

To be sure, the architects of the Nye initiative might have tried harder to assuage Chinese concerns about the renewed security relationship between Japan and the United States, to reduce Japanese concerns regarding the rise of China, and to overcome Japanese domestic resistance to clarified Japanese roles in emergencies. To focus on the shortcomings, however, would be to miss the remarkable progress that the initiative accomplished in a short period. Within just a few years, negotiators on both sides took a relationship that had lost its sense of purpose and instilled in it a new rationale—namely, to provide stability within the region and cooperation in case of emergencies. It helped train a younger generation of officials on both sides on security issues, provided them with a shared understanding, and thereby laid the foundations for a more effective and cooperative military relationship.

Explaining Success

It is not difficult to point to at least some of the reasons for the success of the Nye initiative. It is much harder, however, to judge whether they can be turned into lessons about the conduct of U.S.-Japan negotiations in general or whether they were anomalies born of circumstances that are unlikely to be repeated.

The first reason, which has been emphasized in the preceding account, is perhaps the most instructive: the creation and maintenance of broad support among key groups on both sides. In negotiations between complex, pluralistic democratic polities such as the United States and Japan, policymakers can press ahead with bold proposals only if they have the support of a broad range of key groups. Thus, policymakers and negotiators must make it a priority both to create a sufficiently broad degree of common understanding and shared purpose and to maintain it by keeping all interested parties informed of developments. It is not necessary, or even often desirable, to involve these parties in the negotiations themselves, but it is vital to make each of these parties *feel involved*, to give them confidence that their interests and opinions are represented and respected at the negotiating table.

At a minimum, these constituencies must acquiesce. When explicit concurrence of every party is not possible, tacit acceptance may suffice.

In postwar Japan internal consensus building has long been the vital precursor to effective international negotiation. In the United States, however, the situation is often different. For instance, when President Richard Nixon and National Security Advisor Henry Kissinger moved forward on decisions regarding China in the early 1970s, circumstances permitted a very small group surrounding Kissinger and Nixon to make key decisions. But in the early 1990s when U.S. policymakers turned to the security relationship with Japan, a democratic country, various groups were involved on both sides. Hence the importance to the Nye initiative of enlisting support from such interested parties as the Department of Defense, the U.S. embassy in Tokyo, the White House, Congress, and the community of former officials. At the same time, major institutional resistance to the Pentagon's program had faded by mid-1994, making even low-level involvement in the State Department, and no involvement elsewhere, sufficient for success. Nor was there significant opposition in Congress. This breadth of U.S. backing for the initiative was mirrored on the Japanese side by support from the Japanese embassy in Washington, MOFA, the JDA, the defense tribe of politicians, and an influential group of former officials.

A second ingredient in the success of the Nye initiative, and one hard to reproduce in other U.S.-Japan negotiating encounters, was the personnel involved. On the American side were a number of people who had not only

acquired considerable experience but also developed close working relationships and personal friendships with their counterparts. They were, for
the most part, experts in diplomacy and political-military and strategic relations with Japan. Typical was a small cadre of Japan experts at the
Department of Defense: Paul Giarra had had numerous navy assignments
in Japan and had attended the National Institute for Defense Studies in
Tokyo, Japan's equivalent of the National War College. His deputy and successor, Robin Sakoda, was a U.S. Army foreign area officer with extensive
Japan experience and academic training. Sakoda's predecessor, army major
Rich Douglas, was a West Point graduate in nuclear physics and an Olmsted
Scholar in Japan. Both Mike Green and Patrick Cronin were indispensable,
central players. This lineup of alliance managers may have been no better
or no worse than previous generations of Japan hands. Most significant,
however, was that they were in place and prepared to act when circumstances permitted and strategies required. This long-term investment in
human resources is an essential sunk cost in every successful negotiation
with Japan.

The Americans' close personal and professional relationships with their
Japanese counterparts were complemented by the academic, political, and
bureaucratic standing of Joseph Nye and Ezra Vogel, whose intellectual
reputations and personal relationships with key Japanese elders gave them
enormous credibility in the eyes of the Japanese leadership. Nye, an academic with extensive government service, came to his job as assistant secretary of defense with the priority of reenergizing the security relationship.
Vogel, at the National Intelligence Council, had been well known in Japan
long before this, especially because of his popular book *Japan as Number One*,
published in 1979; he spoke fluent Japanese (as well as Chinese); and he was
addressed with the Japanese honorific *sensei* (teacher) by many of Japan's
political leaders. The late addition, in May 1995, of the catalyst of Kurt
Campbell, Harvard faculty member, Russian scholar, and veteran of the
National Security Council's fight to create the North American Free Trade
Agreement, added tremendous drive and determination to the group. His
just-in-time involvement and dynamic contributions animated the entire
process. Secretary of State Bill Perry's personal interest and involvement
were vital to success, dating from his time as deputy secretary. Without his
close sponsorship, success would not have been possible.

This cadre of alliance managers did their utmost to create an atmosphere of workmanlike collegiality with their Japanese counterparts. The consistent American approach was one of patience and collaboration, laying out requirements and making the case for a stronger alliance to the Japanese side while fighting their own battles within the U.S. bureaucracy.

It was in these bureaucratic battles with other Americans that the U.S. negotiators faced some of their most difficult challenges. Notwithstanding the broad support for the Nye initiative among many key groups, there was also opposition, especially from functional offices within the Department of Defense, expressed in the form of legal obstacles and reluctance to provide operational support that would assuage constant Japanese apprehensions about the American commitment. For instance, the refusal of the U.S. Air Force to transport Japanese peacekeepers to Goma, Zaire, during the Rwandan refugee crisis created a significant breach in Japan's confidence in the United States.

The U.S. negotiators were also handicapped by the relatively low status accorded regional specialists within the U.S. bureaucracy. Whereas the Japanese bureaucracy selects its best and brightest to work on U.S. affairs, able U.S. officials are dispersed to many different areas. Assignments to U.S. military offices in particular were often made in a casual and offhanded manner; simply being in the right place at the right time helped immeasurably to advance an American Japan expert's career. This offhandedness was born of an emphasis within the U.S. armed services on operational assignments and performance rather than on the business of alliance management. Regional specialists in the U.S. military are rarely selected for important line assignments. It is notable that none of the U.S. military officers involved in the Nye initiative were selected for command or promoted; what they did was not valued by their respective services, which tended to regard only service at sea or in the field as deserving of reward.

Like the American side, the Japanese team included many highly experienced diplomats and defense officials. Unlike their American counterparts, however, the negotiators in the JDA were selected and groomed carefully. They usually enjoyed successive seasoning assignments on American affairs and were later promoted to the highest positions in the JDA. It was interesting to note a distinct transformation at the JDA during this period, where the recruiting and morale-building policies of Nishihiro were starting to pay off. The bright young officials from the JDA who had been assigned as visiting senior fellows at NDU and other Washington-area think tanks for several years personified this trend. They began to play a broader part in international security strategic discussions, which until that time had been almost exclusively conducted within MOFA. The joint discussions in 1994–96 helped groom this group of officials.

Japanese diplomats on the fast track were often assigned to the embassy in Washington as either first secretary or minister (and had typically been schooled in the United States or Great Britain), where they were groomed to represent Japan directly to its most important ally. With few exceptions, these Washington alumni formed a cadre who played key roles in Japan's foreign ministry, their fortunes waxing and waning along with MOFA's American school.

With sufficient political cover in place from mid-1994 onward, Japanese officials who had taken part in the joint discussions in 1994–95 were prepared to make many adjustments and to do so quickly in an effort to resolve problems. Takamizawa, for instance, made a notable effort to revise the NDPO in 1994–95 after American protestations. Negotiations in late 1994 over the proposed work plan for the next year proceeded very smoothly. Negotiations with Ishii over changes to the Status of Forces Agreement in October 1995, after the Okinawa rape crisis, went exceptionally well, effectively forestalling the need for structural changes and major revisions to the SOFA.

As usual with the other major agreements, negotiating the specific wording of the Joint Declaration took place late at night in the Foreign Ministry (such hours being an honorable tradition within the Japan bureaucracy) in a pro forma diplomatic exercise, but progress was smooth and the debates were more often over grammar than substance. Each stage in the negotiations was surprisingly easy, given the experience during the Cold War of persistent Japanese resistance to the very idea of Japan shouldering a larger share of the defense burden. In fact, the broad outlines of agreement were in place as early as the end of 1994, when the Work Plan was agreed on.

The personnel on both sides shared an important and unusual distinction that set them apart from most other Japanese and American negotiators: first and foremost they were alliance managers, not adversaries. This commonality drew them together far more than any disagreements or difficult issues could drive them apart. In a sense, the real negotiations were with the respective national bureaucracies, political leaderships, and military hierarchies. The broad strategic discussions in which these alliance managers participated during the Nye initiative not only provided a context in which they could place their detailed work but also strengthened their commitment to the success of their efforts.

This degree of collegiality is impossible to achieve in more competitive contractual discussions, such as those of the U.S.-Japan trade wars from the early 1970s until the mid-1990s. In such adversarial negotiations, sometimes the very same Japanese negotiators who have displayed flexibility on security issues become extremely deliberate and cautious. Ryozo Kato, the dean of MOFA's "American school," is one example. Although renowned for his support of the alliance and for the imaginative innovation and soft-spoken intelligence he displayed in security negotiations, he left a very different impression in the mid- to late 1990s, when he proved a tough and unyielding counterpart during bilateral air transport negotiations.

A third reason for the success of the Nye initiative, and one even harder to replicate than the character of the personnel involved, was the intervention of external events that grabbed the attention of senior decision makers. The Taiwan Strait crisis served to underscore the importance of the U.S.-Japan alliance, while the Okinawa rape crisis not only emphasized the alliance's vulnerability but also seized the attention of the political leadership; both contributed to a readiness to resolve outstanding issues and to reach an agreement that would put the relationship on a firm footing for the future.

Limitations

As we have noted, the success of the Nye initiative in negotiating the Joint Declaration has not been matched by subsequent success in using that document to clarify and bolster the military relationship between the two countries. Most of the time reasons for this failure have little to do with the conduct of the initiative itself. Instead, they are related to Japanese dependence on ambiguity on the international stage, to a lack of continued high-level U.S. attention to Japanese security matters after President Clinton's visit to Tokyo in 1996, and to political transition in Japan.

In one respect, however, the way in which the security negotiations were conducted did contribute to the failure to build on the Joint Declaration. Indeed, this reason for failure was also a reason for the earlier success of the initiative: namely, the crucial role played by a few key individuals. Nye and Vogel were the architects of the initiative and were instrumental in building and maintaining the broad-ranging support it enjoyed and that underpinned its eventual success. But they did not remain in government long after the signing of the Joint Declaration. Vogel left Washington in August 1995 to return to Harvard as Henry Ford II Professor of the Social Sciences and director of the Fairbank Center for East Asian Research. When Nye departed in December 1995, lured back to Harvard to be the dean of the Kennedy School of Government, Japan issues lost their primary champion in the Pentagon. The U.S. team, under the direction of Kurt Campbell, continued as energetically as before, but Campbell lacked the broad support necessary to press ahead on concrete issues. With Secretary Perry's retirement a year later, he lost his senior political patron.

During 1991–95, negotiations had three carefully laminated layers: political, bureaucratic, and military. Efforts on these three levels were carefully coordinated to maximize coherence and enhance leadership. This coordination did not survive the departure of Vogel, Nye, and Perry. Subsequently, military and civilian policies began to diverge in both Japan and the United States. If there is a lesson in this, it is that a bold initiative can enjoy long- as well as short-term success only if great care is taken and great investment is made in creating and nurturing a political, bureaucratic, and strategic framework able to sustain and advance the new relationships and new expectations created by that initiative.

Finally, no initiative or cadre is better than its time and circumstances. These negotiations succeeded, in the final analysis, because each side was prepared to exploit the opportunities it was dealt by domestic politics, bureaucratic leadership, external events, and ideas whose time had come.

Appendix

The following is the full text of the Japan-U.S. Joint Declaration on Security Alliance issued April 17, 1996, after a summit meeting between Prime Minister Ryutaro Hashimoto and President Bill Clinton.

Japan-U.S. Joint Declaration on Security Alliance for the 21st Century

1. Today, the Prime Minister and the President celebrated one of the most successful bilateral relationships in history. The leaders took pride in the profound and positive contribution this relationship has made to world peace and regional stability and prosperity. The strong Alliance between Japan and the United States helped ensure peace and security in the Asia-Pacific region during the Cold War. Our Alliance continues to underlie the dynamic economic growth in this region. The two leaders agreed that the future security and prosperity of both Japan and the United States are tied inextricably to the future of the Asia-Pacific region.

The benefits of peace and prosperity that spring from the Alliance are due not only to the commitments of the two governments, but also to the contributions of the Japanese and American people who have shared the burden of securing freedom and democracy. The Prime Minister and the President expressed their profound gratitude to those who sustain the Alliance, especially those Japanese communities that host U.S. Forces, and those Americans who, far from home, devote themselves to the defense of peace and freedom.

2. For more than a year, the two governments conducted an intensive review of the evolving political and security environment of the Asia-Pacific region and of various aspects of the Japan-U.S. security relationship. On the basis of this review, the Prime Minister and the President reaffirmed their commitment to the profound common values that guide our national policies: the maintenance of freedom, the pursuit of democracy and respect for human rights. They agreed that the foundations for our cooperation remain firm, and that this partnership will remain vital in the twenty-first century.

THE REGIONAL OUTLOOK

3. Since the end of the Cold War, the possibility of global armed conflict has receded. The last few years have seen expanded political and security dialogue among countries of the region. Respect for democratic principles is growing. Prosperity is more widespread than at any other time in history, and we are witnessing the emergence of an Asia-Pacific community. The Asia-Pacific region has become the most dynamic area of the globe.

At the same time, instability and uncertainty persist in the region. Tensions continue on the Korean Peninsula. There are still heavy concentrations of military forces, including nuclear arsenals. Unresolved territorial disputes, potential regional conflicts, and the proliferation of weapons of mass destruction and their means of delivery all constitute sources of instability.

THE JAPAN-U.S. ALLIANCE AND THE TREATY OF MUTUAL COOPERATION AND SECURITY

4. The Prime Minister and the President underscored the importance of promoting stability in this region and dealing with the security challenges facing both countries.

In this regard, the Prime Minister and the President reiterated the significant value of the Alliance between Japan and the United States. They reaffirmed that the Japan-U.S. security relationship, based on the Treaty of Mutual Cooperation and Security between Japan and the United States of America, remains the cornerstone for achieving common security objectives and for maintaining a stable and prosperous environment for the Asia-Pacific region as we enter the 21st century.

(a) The Prime Minister confirmed Japan's fundamental defense policy as articulated in its new "National Defense Program Outline" adopted in November 1995, which underscored that the Japanese defense capabilities should play appropriate roles in the security environment after the Cold War. The Prime Minister and the President agreed that the most effective framework for the defense of Japan is close defense cooperation between the two countries. This cooperation is based on a combination of appropriate defense capabilities for the Self-Defense Forces of Japan and the Japan-U.S. security arrangements. The leaders again confirmed that U.S. deterrence under the Treaty of Mutual Cooperation and Security remains the guarantee for Japan's security.

(b) The Prime Minister and the President agreed that continued U.S. military presence is also essential for preserving peace and stability in the Asia-Pacific region. The leaders shared the common recognition that the Japan-U.S. security relationship forms an essential pillar which supports the positive regional engagement of the U.S.

The President emphasized the U.S. commitment to the defense of Japan as well as to peace and stability in the Asia-Pacific region. He noted that there has been some adjustment of U.S. forces in the Asia-Pacific region since the end of the Cold War. On the basis of a thorough assessment, the United States reaffirmed that meeting its commitments in the prevailing security environment requires the maintenance of its current force structure of about 100,000 forward deployed military personnel in the region, including about the current level in Japan.

(c) The Prime Minister welcomed the U.S. determination to remain a stable and steadfast presence in the region. He reconfirmed that Japan would continue appropriate contributions for the maintenance of U.S. forces in Japan, such as through the provision of facilities and areas in accordance with the Treaty of Mutual Cooperation and Security and Host Nation Support. The President expressed U.S. appreciation for Japan's contributions and welcomed the conclusion of the new Special Measures Agreement, which provides financial support for U.S. forces stationed in Japan.

BILATERAL COOPERATION UNDER THE
JAPAN-U.S. SECURITY RELATIONSHIP

5. The Prime Minister and the President, with the objective of enhancing the credibility of this vital security relationship, agreed to undertake efforts to advance cooperation in the following areas.

(a) Recognizing that close bilateral defense cooperation is a central element of the Japan-U.S. alliance, both governments agreed that continued close consultation is essential. Both governments will further enhance the exchange of information and views on the international situation, in particular the Asia-Pacific region. At the same time, in response to the changes which may arise in the international security environment, both governments will continue to consult closely on defense policies and military postures, including the U.S. force structure in Japan, which will best meet their requirements.

(b) The Prime Minister and the President agreed to initiate a review of the 1978 Guidelines for Japan-U.S. Defense Cooperation to build upon the close working relationship already established between Japan and the United States.

The two leaders agreed on the necessity to promote bilateral policy coordination, including studies on bilateral cooperation in dealing with situations that may emerge in the areas surrounding Japan and which will have an important influence on the peace and security of Japan.

(c) The Prime Minister and the President welcomed the April 15, 1996, signature of the Agreement Between the Government of Japan and the Government of the United States of America Concerning Reciprocal Provision of Logistic Support, Supplies and Services Between the Self-Defense Forces of Japan and the Armed Forces of the United States of America, and expressed their hope that this Agreement will further promote the bilateral cooperative relationship.

(d) Noting the importance of interoperability in all facets of cooperation between the Self-Defense Forces of Japan and the U.S. forces, the two governments will enhance mutual exchange in the areas of technology and equipment, including bilateral cooperative research and development of equipment such as the support fighter (F-2).

(e) The two governments recognized that the proliferation of weapons of mass destruction and their means of delivery has important implications for their common security. They will work together to prevent proliferation and will continue to cooperate in the ongoing study on ballistic missile defense.

6. The Prime Minister and the President recognized that the broad support and understanding of the Japanese people are indispensable for the smooth stationing of U.S. forces in Japan, which is the core element of the Japan-U.S. security arrangements. The two leaders agreed that both governments will make every effort to deal with various issues related to the presence and status of U.S. forces. They also agreed to make further efforts to enhance mutual understanding between U.S. forces and local Japanese communities.

In particular, with respect to Okinawa, where U.S. facilities and areas are highly concentrated, the Prime Minister and the President reconfirmed their determination to carry out steps to consolidate, realign, and reduce U.S. facilities and areas consistent with the objectives of the Treaty of Mutual Cooperation and Security. In this respect, the two leaders took satisfaction in the significant progress which has been made so far through the "Special Action Committee on Okinawa" (SACO) and welcomed the far reaching measures outlined in the SACO Interim Report of April 15, 1996. They expressed their firm commitment to achieve a successful conclusion of the SACO process by November 1996.

REGIONAL COOPERATION

7. The Prime Minister and the President agreed that the two governments will jointly and individually strive to achieve a more peaceful and stable security environment in the Asia-Pacific region. In this regard, the two leaders recognized that the engagement of the United States in the region, supported by the Japan-U.S. security relationship, constitutes the foundation for such efforts.

The two leaders stressed the importance of peaceful resolution of problems in the region. They emphasized that it is extremely important for the stability and prosperity of the region that China play a positive and constructive role, and, in this context, stressed the interest of both countries in furthering cooperation with China. Russia's ongoing process of reform contributes to regional and global stability, and merits continued encouragement and cooperation. The leaders also stated that full normalization of Japan-Russia relations based on the Tokyo Declaration is important to peace and stability in the Asia-Pacific region. They noted also that stability on the Korean Peninsula is vitally important to Japan and the United States and reaffirmed that both countries will continue to make every effort in this regard, in close cooperation with the Republic of Korea.

The Prime Minister and the President reaffirmed that the two governments will continue working jointly and with other countries in the region to further develop multilateral regional security dialogues and cooperation mechanisms such as the ASEAN Regional Forum, and eventually, security dialogues regarding Northeast Asia.

GLOBAL COOPERATION

8. The Prime Minister and the President recognized that the Treaty of Mutual Cooperation and Security is the core of the Japan-U.S. Alliance, and underlies the mutual confidence that constitutes the foundation for bilateral cooperation on global issues.

The Prime Minister and the President agreed that the two governments will strengthen their cooperation in support of the United Nations and other international organizations through activities such as peacekeeping and humanitarian relief operations.

Both governments will coordinate their policies and cooperate on issues such as arms control and disarmament, including acceleration of the Comprehensive Test Ban Treaty (CTBT) negotiations and the prevention of the proliferation of weapons of mass destruction and their means of delivery. The two leaders agreed that cooperation in the United Nations and APEC, and on issues such as the North Korean nuclear problem, the Middle East peace process, and the peace implementation process in the former Yugoslavia, helps to build the kind of world that promotes our shared interests and values.

CONCLUSION

9. In concluding the Prime Minister and the President agreed that the three legs of the Japan-U.S. relationship—security, political and economic—are based on shared values and interests and rest on the mutual confidence embodied in the Treaty of Mutual Cooperation and Security. The Prime Minister and the President reaffirmed their strong determination, on the eve of the twenty-first century, to build on the successful history of security cooperation and to work hand-in-hand to secure peace and prosperity for future generations.

CONCLUSIONS

Patrick M. Cronin

The quartet of case studies in Japanese negotiating behavior that make up this volume will resonate with any American official who has negotiated with the government of Japan on either trade or security issues. Together, Michael Blaker, Ezra Vogel, and Paul Giarra have created a multifaceted and instantly recognizable portrait of Japanese negotiating style, one in which the key features are much in evidence: the Japanese tendency toward reactive and defensive "coping"; the need for crisis and external pressure, or *gaiatsu*, to force and empower a final top-level official to close a deal; the emphasis on thorough preparation, or *nemawashi*, and internal consensus building; the use of back-channel talks to float trial balloons or advance new ideas to move a sterile official process; the step-by-tiny-step approach or the protracted parsing of issues into finite details and infinite discussions; the figurative or literal sucking of teeth in reaction to abrupt changes of position or perceived major U.S. demands; and a desire for confidentiality, even secrecy, until all aspects of a negotiation have been concluded.

In addition to providing original analyses of specific case studies of negotiation, the authors of this volume achieve three objectives. First, they add to our general knowledge about Japanese negotiating behavior, carefully supporting their generalizations with empirical evidence. Second, they provide an excellent opportunity for reflecting on U.S. negotiating behavior. Finally, they underscore the importance of effective negotiations across cultural boundaries in the peaceful conduct of international affairs.

In describing U.S. negotiations with Japan over orange and rice imports, the production of the FSX fighter aircraft, and the redefinition of the security alliance for the post–Cold War era, the authors reveal several recurring patterns of Japanese negotiating style.

DEFENSIVE COPING

The case studies support Michael Blaker's thesis that, for most Japanese officials, diplomacy is a risk-reducing endeavor in which avoiding potential loss of face is the overriding imperative. The reader can easily understand the consternation that a negotiator from the Ministry of Agriculture may have felt on hearing American demands for open competition in Japan's near-sacred domestic rice market, or a negotiator from the Japanese Defense Agency or MITI (the Ministry of International Trade and Industry, now known as METI) on being pressured by Washington to accept an existing American fighter rather than develop a new Japanese design.

Blaker's term "coping" to describe Japan's overall approach to negotiation is particularly apt. In English the verb *cope* denotes successfully contending with a problem; but its etymology (from the French *coup*, a blow—which in turn derives from the Greek *kolaphos*) suggests doing so by striking with a fist. Japan's tendency to be reactive is seldom matched by passivity. Instead, Japanese negotiators are effective managers of active defense. From testing the waters to warily but thoroughly sizing up a negotiating context, to methodically weighing and sorting out options, to deferring action, to crafting consensus within an agency or ministry, to preempting criticism, to finding ways to adapt with minimal risk, the Japanese government is a model of hyperactive incrementalism in negotiations.

Even on subjects that would seem to be win-win issues for both the United States and Japan, such as reaffirming the alliance, Japanese negotiators frequently adopt the defensive posture of reacting to American positions and demands. They may first try to slow down the tempo of the negotiating process or minimize the issue under discussion to allow for an internal Japanese consensus to cohere, at least within critical parts of the bureaucracy, and, subsequently, to gather the political will to codify agreements at the highest level.

Once Japan has settled into a pattern of behavior, it is reluctant to change and resists efforts to make it do so. This defensiveness is accentuated in cases where an existing pattern has previously enjoyed U.S.

approval or at least acceptance. For instance, in the 1950s and early 1960s the United States was content for the Japanese market to remain relatively closed. When the United States began to press Japan to open its market in the mid-1960s, Japan resisted strongly.

USE OF GAIATSU

Japan's penchant for "playing defense" in negotiations explains why external pressure—*gaiatsu*—is needed to prod the Japanese into shifting position. As Blaker puts it, *gaiatsu* "is the straw that stirs the drink in Japanese-American negotiations." It was just such pressure that convinced Prime Minister Fukuda he would have to risk a political assault from Japan's farm lobby by quadrupling foreign orange imports. Similarly, pressure from Deputy Secretary of State Lawrence Eagleburger and other U.S. officials eventually convinced Tokyo that partial access to Japan's rice market would not satisfy Washington. Conversely, when Secretary of Defense Casper Weinberger failed to apply pressure on Koichi Kato with respect to the FSX fighter, the Japanese may have been misled into concluding that Washington did not care whether the aircraft was of Japanese design.

The Japanese seem especially sensitive to pressure that threatens to isolate Japan, as when American negotiators emphasize the enormous stake Japan has in maintaining its close security alliance with the United States; or, as in the case of rice, when they threaten to multilateralize an issue, thereby drawing Japan into a possible dispute with other members of the international community.

CONSENSUS BUILDING

All four cases clearly demonstrate the overriding importance the Japanese attach to consensus building. Within Japanese society as a whole, as noted in the introductory chapter, *wa* (harmony) is highly prized, yet fiercely competitive groups at every societal level are always threatening to disrupt that harmony. Thus, the Japanese have to try to accommodate the interests of these self-assertive groups, building consensus through a process of informal but extensive consultation before taking action—a process known as *nemawashi*.

By the time a Japanese negotiating team sits down with its counterparts, numerous government agencies, politicians, and interest groups have been consulted and a consensus has been painstakingly forged on the issue to be negotiated and the position to be adopted by Japan's negotiating team. If new issues arise during the diplomatic negotiation, or if the other side makes demands that exceed the scope of the internally arranged consensus, the Japanese team can do little except reiterate its position or return home while a new consensus is built.

One result of this approach is that the substance and the process of negotiation are often severed from one another, and formal negotiation sessions are treated as little more than venues for official posturing and explanation rather than substantive give-and-take. This can make Japanese "negotiating behavior" seem almost an oxymoron. Whereas American negotiators conceive of negotiating, in its simplest form, as a dialectical process—two competing views clashing to reach a compromise—the Japanese tend to see negotiation as the art of explanation, attempting to bring outsiders to understand and accommodate an unyielding internal consensus. The 1988 agreement on orange imports, for instance, was struck not at the bargaining table but in Japanese political circles, where Prime Minister Takeshita adroitly engineered a deal to meet American demands. When a fundamental agreement in principle has been made, however, Japanese negotiators appear ready and able to compromise on details, as was the case in the final phase of talks over rice imports. Once the main issue of a phase-in period before tariffication took effect had been settled, the Japanese readily agreed to split the difference between the two sides' proposed levels of access during the interim period. In the case of FSX, it was the politician Ozawa and the LDP defense *zoku* rather than negotiators at the table that forced the final breakthrough to an agreement.

Japanese negotiation, therefore, is a segmented, incremental process. Information about American views is collected and fed back to Tokyo, contributing to the construction of an internal consensus in private. By the time formal negotiations occur, Japanese negotiation turns into mere explanation and the deflection of opposing views. Thus, the American official who gets on a plane headed for Narita International Airport hoping to negotiate a new accord on market access or defense cooperation will almost surely be disappointed if he or she is looking for quick agreement—

irrespective of the terms. The different conceptions of negotiating process held by U.S. and Japanese officials are a perennial source of friction, because Americans tend to see Japanese unwillingness to compromise on their feet, so to speak, as defensive conservatism, whereas the Japanese tend to see formal negotiation as the result of a failure of the social contract in Japan that requires step-by-step consensus building rather than a disputatious confrontation over alternative ideas.

BACK CHANNELS

Another theme of Japanese negotiating behavior that is echoed throughout these case studies is the frequent use of back-channel communications and unofficial "track-two" venues to air ideas, provide a sounding board, overcome impasses, and establish a framework or vision for the subsequent course of negotiations. This pattern, of course, is not unique to the Japanese. Back-room deal making has a long tradition in American political practice—even if it coexists with the Wilsonian idealistic tradition of "open covenants openly arrived at." What seems to be distinctive about the Japanese negotiating style is the degree of reliance on private channels to advance a number of goals at different stages of talks.

Private channels are used, first, in the prenegotiating phase to survey opinion and exhaustively assess the views of U.S. policymakers and those who might influence them, such as think-tank analysts and former officials. Second, back channels are employed to reach an agreement in principle in a quasi-official or unofficial setting without the involvement of a large, semipublic audience (as when, for example, the Japanese privately explored the U.S. views on what level of Japanese orange import quotas was acceptable, and when they postulated new defense guidelines at sessions with National Defense University personnel rather than directly with the Pentagon). A third use of back channels is the dispatching of official and unofficial delegations to explain to U.S. audiences why Japan is constrained from accepting American demands or why the lack of internal consensus on an issue has prevented progress in bilateral discussions. A fourth use is the high-level, back-channel communications in which the president and prime minister, or their select representatives, close a deal—as was the case on rice—by making concessions hitherto considered impossible.

Sometimes business interests provide a valuable back channel. In the second round of negotiations over oranges, for example, the back-channel role was largely played by Fujii Trading Company and Sunkist, the business interests with the largest stakes in a deal. On other occasions, senior officials proffered "unofficial" concepts to help break an impasse. Thus, when Assistant Secretary of Defense Richard Armitage proposed joint development of FSX on either the F-18 or F-16 design, while agreeing to have a Japanese firm serve as the prime contractor, he was skillfully circumventing the bogged-down official process. Similarly, while officials in Washington and Tokyo had much difficulty in conducting a 2+2 meeting of the top defense and foreign affairs officials from the two countries, strategic dialogue was able to proceed relatively unimpeded through track-two meetings. At the same time, Tokyo undoubtedly found an unofficial venue such as the National Defense University helpful because it empowered the U.S. Department of Defense over those interests in Washington that had been focused on pursuing trade interests—even at the expense of the security relationship—during the early period of the Clinton administration.

SLOW PACE

Japanese negotiators seem to feel relatively unconstrained by time pressures in the early and middle stages of a negotiation. Whereas U.S. officials are habitually in a hurry to reach the bottom line, the Japanese approach new negotiations with a view to buying time, which will allow for comprehensive preparation and domestic consensus building. Negotiations in Japan are usually in the hands of ministries that have permanent officials; these officials feel that they can wait out the four-year presidential cycle in the United States, and that they can work according to a long-term strategy that is subject to fewer changes than the strategies formulated by successive administrations in the United States.

One of the pioneers of research in culture and communication, Raymond Cohen, has observed that, in general, traditional societies have all the time in the world; the natural order, not human activity, determines the rhythm of events. In contrast, Cohen labels the U.S. approach as "monochronic," pursuing one thing at a time, with schedules and deadlines looming large.[1] The pattern of Japanese negotiators frequently needing two to three months to prepare for an official negotiating round bespeaks their felt need to be well prepared, to ensure that no surprises cause a sudden loss of face, to be in a position to explain the internal consensus in Japan—or, on occasion, to offer noncommittal diplomatic language to cover the absence of such a consensus and thus buy more time. In the early stage of talks over rice imports, for example, Japanese negotiators employed a number of tactics to avoid discussing the issues. Blaker notes that the Japanese often use silence as a tactic for delaying, buying time, and fending off American demands.

A multitude of diplomatic iterations takes time, of course, something that American negotiators often find annoying, especially because the American rhythm of negotiation is closely calibrated to the electoral calendar and to the even more limited tenure of senior political appointees. The more that America's Japan hands, in the U.S. embassy in Tokyo or on the Japan desk in the State or Defense Department, urge patience to busy U.S. officials, the more they risk being perceived as part of the problem. When Americans stay engaged in a vital negotiation, however, this friction may provoke a denouement in which senior officials step in to resolve a perceived crisis.

Paradoxically, in some circumstances the slow pace of negotiating can work against the Japanese, who may fail to anticipate how their American interlocutors' goals, demands, and tactics may change over time. Japanese foot-dragging sometimes proves detrimental to a negotiation, inadvertently adding to the shock effect on officials in Tokyo. While Japan takes months to formulate a carefully agreed-on position in Tokyo, Washington may move on its own clock and start over with a fresh position or revised statement of demands. At various points in each of the four cases presented here, Japanese interlocutors found themselves confronted with a new U.S. position or demand, seemingly casting aside prior expectations or even understandings. This pattern of "moving the goalposts" is not uncommon in American policymaking, and Japanese negotiators seeking to hew to agreed-to positions over long periods of time can find that the United States has abruptly changed the terms of the negotiation.

In the final stages of negotiation, time becomes a political lever in Japan. Just as time pressure and high-level summits tend to push bureaucracies into overdrive, the time-sensitive sense of crisis, or *kikikan*, in negotiations has tended to force or allow a Japanese political figure, often the prime minister, to broker a compromise beyond a previously unimaginable position. If it is done well, both sides can find such a deal mutually beneficial and politically advantageous. But sometimes a Japanese government that fails to say "No" and closes a deal under American pressure can produce a nationalistic backlash, which in turn fuels resentment in the United States over the failure of the Japanese political leaders to convince their public that the compromise is in Japan's interest.

CONFIDENTIALITY

Japanese negotiating behavior tends to exhibit a strong desire for confidentiality, punctuated or followed by carefully scripted public explanations of selected details regarding a likely final decision or a description of how a decision was reached. Secrecy is vital for private, quiet understandings that may help break an impasse, lest a premature deal leak out before an internal consensus of support has been built in Japan. Hence, Prime Minister Hosokawa was obsessed with keeping secret Japan's intention to accede to American demands to open the domestic market to foreign rice. Such attempts at keeping an agreement confidential until the last minute not only failed but also may have added to Hosokawa's lack of support in Japan once the controversial accord was made public. In contrast, Prime Minister Nakasone used a public statement about Japan's likely accession to U.S. requests over the FSX deal to signal that Japan had been worn down by two and a half years of pressure from the Pentagon and Congress. Thus, while public pronouncements can be useful in pushing forward a negotiation, in general the Japanese prefer to keep the details of talks and even the outcome secret until the entire deal has been concluded. For instance, Japanese officials did not reveal the precise details of the alliance reaffirmation until a widely publicized summit meeting.

Our leaders often fail to assess their counterparts' negotiating style or to understand them. In similar fashion, even when Japanese prepare thoroughly for negotiations, they can misinterpret or be shocked by changes in the U.S. approach or in U.S. demands. Defining culture is an elusive art, which is why many experts such as Raymond Cohen prefer an ostensive approach to help show its complex contours. So, too, with a national style of negotiation. At the end of the day, the purpose of this volume and the United States Institute of Peace's cross-cultural negotiation project is to help widen our appreciation of ways in which other countries' negotiating styles are distinctive and how they differ from that which many American negotiators bring to the bargaining table. An assumption of the cross-cultural negotiation project is that negotiators are unlikely to be very successful in international negotiations unless they know well at least one other national approach to negotiation. As the initiator of the project, Institute president Richard Solomon, wrote in his seminal study of Chinese negotiating behavior: "The objective of the project is to penetrate the veil of mystery—or at least of unfamiliarity—surrounding different cultures and to remove the uncertainty that can confound American—or other foreign—diplomats and nongovernmental negotiators when dealing with unfamiliar countries and counterparts, thus clearing the way for more productive negotiating encounters."[2]

We are one humanity in an ever smaller world, but within that world is great cultural diversity, some of which can be usefully broken down along national lines even in an increasingly borderless world of globalization. This problem—the impetus for the United States Institute of Peace to sponsor a series of country studies as part of its cross-cultural negtiation project—is an old one. The cultural anthropologist Ruth Benedict, asked during World War II to explain the Japanese, concluded that the Japanese were a complex mixture of both the chrysanthemum and the sword, of aesthetics and militarism:

> One of the handicaps of the twentieth century is that we still have the vaguest and most biased notions, not only of what makes Japan a nation of Japanese, but of what makes the United States a nation of Americans, France a nation of Frenchmen, and Russia a nation of Russians. Lacking this knowledge, each country misunderstands the other. We fear irreconcilable differences when the trouble is only between Tweedledum and Tweedledee, and we talk about common purposes when one nation by virtue of its whole experience and system of values has in mind a quite different course of action from the one we meant. We do not give ourselves a chance to find out what their

habits and values are. If we did, we might discover that a course of action is not necessarily vicious because it is not the one we know.[3]

Of course, to find recurring patterns in a national negotiating style is not to point to permanent tendencies so much as to underscore prevailing proclivities. For one thing, the tendencies are the result not just of culture, as pointed out in the introduction to this volume, but also of historical situations and national institutions. Political environments change—and in the past fifteen years they have changed with unusual speed, in the process causing both Americans and Japanese to revise their opinions of themselves and of each other. And institutions also change—witness the current debate in Japan over giving the prime minister greater power and the decision in the fall of 2001 to allow the Self-Defense Force to play a more active role in missions outside Japan. The future of U.S.-Japanese relations is unpredictable, but it is sure to involve increasing layers of complexity, both because of myriad multilateral as well as bilateral negotiations and because of the increasing impact of local politics, civil society, and nongovernmental organizations on international relations. Trade issues in an era of globalization increasingly have multilateral implications. And security issues— from preserving peace on the Korean Peninsula to considering the future of bases in Okinawa—necessarily involve numerous actors.

The handicap to cross-cultural understanding that Ruth Benedict identified more than half a century ago endures in the new century, but it is to be hoped that this volume—and the other books in this series—will go some way toward dispelling ignorance and replacing it with a modicum of understanding of the cultural dynamics that shape negotiating encounters. For specialists, the assessments presented here might appear simplistic, but one must distinguish between simplification and successful synthesis. While four case studies of specific negotiations are too few to permit definitive conclusions about something as complex as national negotiating styles, no number would satisfy the quixotic search for prediction in human behavior. The purpose here has not been to offer a stereotype of Japanese official behavior in negotiations with the United States over trade and security issues. Instead, it has been to sample some of the texture, rhythm, and patterns of those negotiations, with the hope that tomorrow's negotiators will enter talks with greater understanding and sensitivity to Japanese culture.

NOTES

INTRODUCTION

1. Harold Nicolson, *Diplomacy* (New York: Oxford University Press, 1950).

2. Richard H. Solomon, *Chinese Negotiating Behavior: Pursuing Interests through "Old Friends"* (Washington, D.C.: United States Institute of Peace Press, 1999); Jerrold L. Schecter, *Russian Negotiating Behavior: Continuity and Transition* (Washington, D.C.: United States Institute of Peace Press, 1998); Scott Snyder, *Negotiating on the Edge: North Korean Negotiating Behavior* (Washington, D.C.: United States Institute of Peace Press, 1999); and W. R. Smyser, *How Germans Negotiate: Logical Goals, Practical Solutions* (Washington, D.C.: United States Institute of Peace Press, 2002). Charles Cogan's study, *French Negotiating Behavior: Dealing with "La Grande Nation,"* will be published in 2003. The United States Institute of Peace has also published several special reports that focus on national negotiating styles, including *U.S. Negotiating Behavior*, which appeared in October 2002.

3. Among the best books on the subject are Kitamura Hiroshi, Ryohei Murata, and Hisahiko Okazaki, *Between Friends: Japanese Diplomats Look at Japan-U.S. Relations* (New York: Weatherhill, 1985); Robert A. Scalapino, ed., *The Foreign Policy of Japan* (Berkeley, Calif.: University of California Press, 1977); Michael Green, *Japan's Reluctant Realism: Foreign Policy Challenges in an Era of Uncertain Power* (New York: Palgrave, 2001); and Yoichi Funabashi, *Alliance Adrift* (New York: Council on Foreign Relations, 1999).

4. Kevin Avruch thus defines "local cultures" in his book *Culture and Conflict Resolution* (Washington, D.C.: United States Institute of Peace Press, 1998), 10. See also P. W. Black and K. Avruch, "Some Issues in Thinking about Culture and the Resolution of Conflict," *Humanity and Society* 13, no. 1 (1989): 187–194.

5. See "Japan's Internationalization," *U.S. Business News,* January 1, 1986.

1. NEGOTIATIONS ON ORANGE IMPORTS, 1977—88

1. Other accounts of Japanese bargaining on agriculture include Michael R. Reich, Yasuo Endo, and C. Peter Timmer, "Agriculture: The Political Economy of Structural Change," in *America vs. Japan*, ed. Thomas K. McCraw (Boston: Harvard Business School Press, 1986), 155–160; Hideo Sato and Timothy J. Curran, "Agricultural Trade: The Case of Beef and Citrus," in *Coping with U.S.-Japanese Economic Conflicts*, ed. I. M. Destler and Hideo Sato (Lexington, Mass.: D. C. Heath, 1982), 172–177; Gilbert R. Winham, *International Trade and the Tokyo Round Negotiation* (Princeton, N.J.: Princeton University Press, 1986), 324–332; and Haruhiro Fukui, "The GATT Tokyo Round: The Bureaucratic Politics of Multilateral Diplomacy," in *The Politics of Trade*, ed. Michael Blaker (New York: Columbia University, East Asian Institute, 1978), 134–137.

2. Atsushi Kusano, *Nichi-Bei orenji kosho* [Japan-U.S. orange negotiations](Tokyo: Nihon keizai shimbun sha, 1983), 26.

3. Ibid., 28.

4. Ibid., 29.

5. *Nihon keizai shimbun*, November 29, 1977.

6. Tatsuo Takeda, *Nihon no gaiko* [Japanese diplomacy] (Tokyo: Simul Press, 1990), 191.

7. *Asahi shimbun*, September 4, 1994. The SII (or "sigh" to beleaguered Japanese delegates) negotiations commenced in September 1985, advanced laboriously over nearly five years, and ended with a final report in June 1990. This ambitious "initiative" (replaced with the flaccid term "discussion" by skittish Japanese officials) of the Bush Sr. administration targeted over two hundred obstacles in Japan's economic system (e.g., *keiretsu*—a network of businesses that own stakes in one another as a means of mutual security; bid-rigging; and nontransparency in financial markets). The SII package approach, like the earlier Reagan-sponsored, market-oriented, sector-specific (MOSS) strategy and the subsequent "Framework for a New Economic Partnership" of the Clinton years, reflected the trade deficit–inspired shift in U.S. trade strategy from bargaining with Japan on single issues such as citrus products or textiles to omnibus proposals aimed at what U.S. officials considered to be the underlying, fundamental Japanese barriers to foreign trade.

8. Kusano, *Nichi-Bei orenji kosho*, 30–31.

9. Ibid., 94.

10. Ibid., 29–30.

11. Ibid., 31.

12. Ibid., 33; Mark Manyin, "Breaking the Silence: Japan's Behavior in the Tokyo and Uruguay Rounds of the GATT" (Ph.D. diss., Fletcher School of Law and Diplomacy, 1999), 12–13.

13. Higashi Chikara, *Japanese Trade Policy Formulation* (New York: Praeger, 1983), 99; Kusano, *Nichi-Bei orenji kosho*, 93.

14. Kusano, *Nichi-Bei orenji kosho*, 33.

15. Sato and Curran, "Agricultural Trade," 139.

16. Kusano, *Nichi-Bei orenji kosho*, 94.

17. Sato and Curran, "Agricultural Trade," 142–143; Kusano, *Nichi-Bei orenji kosho*, 33, 47.

18. Fujita Eiichi, *Amerika no yomikata; Nihon no ikikata* [The American way of thinking; the Japanese way of life] (Tokyo: Keizaikai, 1986), p. 67; Sato and Curran, "Agricultural Trade," 143.

19. Kusano, *Nichi-Bei orenji kosho*, 35.

20. Ibid., 97–98.

21. Ibid., 45.

22. Ibid., 47.

23. Ibid., 48.

24. Sato and Curran, "Agricultural Trade," 167–170.

25. *Nihon nogyo shimbun*, July 15, 1978, as quoted by Kusano, *Nichi-Bei orenji kosho*, 98–99.

26. Sato and Curran, "Agricultural Trade," 171; Kusano, *Nichi-Bei orenji kosho*, 96.

27. *Nihon nogyo shimbun*, September 12, 1978, as quoted by Kusano, *Nichi-Bei orenji kosho*, 50.

28. Kusano, *Nichi-Bei orenji kosho*, 221.

29. Ibid., 31, 220–221. The Japanese willingness to accept progressively higher import quotas can be explained in part by effective lobbying by Fujii Trading Company, the Japanese agent for California's Sunkist Growers and the dominant firm *(gyosha)* in the business of importing oranges into Japan. The firm's president, Kazuo Fujii, was well connected politically to a handful of top Liberal Democratic politicians whom he cultivated aggressively. Along with providing generous financial contributions to these Diet members, he sometimes added expensive gifts, the most notorious of which was a racehorse he once gave to Ichiro Kono when Kono was minister of agriculture.

Even though his political party connections gave him much indirect influence on government bureaucrats, Fujii went further than that. Not only did he seek favored treatment for his business through cultivating relationships with politicians; he also directly (and excessively in their view) lobbied selected ranking bureaucrats in MITI and Agriculture. If MITI and

Agriculture Ministry officials had acted against Fujii's interests, they would have had to answer to the politicians Fujii had in his pocket.

Across the Pacific, Sunkist served in effect as the vehicle for promoting Fujii's interests with the American government. Blocking liberalization of oranges served both firms' purposes, because liberalization would have brought the heavy-hitting Japanese trading firms into the competition, as had happened when the market for grapefruit and lemons was liberalized. Barring entirely or restricting as much as possible Florida-grown oranges, especially during the May–June period when Florida's citrus would be most competitive, were other goals the two firms had in common. Without Florida fruit and without new firms licensed to compete, the two companies stood to reap a windfall, with a 25 percent share of a far larger market pie once import-quota levels were raised.

30. See Sato and Curran, "Agricultural Trade," 170–172; Kusano, *Nichi-Bei orenji kosho*, 53–55.

31. Reich, Endo, and Timmer, "Agriculture," 175–180; MITI, *Tsusho hakusho* [White paper on trade], *1983–1988;* Susan MacKnight, *JEI Report* 12B (March 28, 1986), 14B (April 8, 1988), 18B (May 6, 1988), and 42A (November 4, 1988).

2. NEGOTIATIONS ON RICE IMPORTS, 1986—93

1. Frank Gibney, "The View from Japan," *Foreign Affairs* 50, no. 3 (October 1971): 101.

2. See Hidezo Inaba and Toyoaki Ikuta, *Nichi-Bei sen'i kosho* [U.S.-Japan textile negotiations] (Tokyo: Kinzoku zaisei jiho kenkyu kai, 1970), 119–147.

3. David Sanger, "Japan's Sensitivity on Rice Issue," *New York Times,* October 28, 1988; Damon Darlin, "Japan Firmly Resists U.S. Pressure on Rice," *Wall Street Journal,* November 12, 1988; *Yomiuri shimbun,* October 30, 1988.

4. *Los Angeles Times,* January 21, 1987.

5. Yeutter warned: "If Japan does not demonstrate its commitment by early December at the Montreal Uruguay Round meetings, we shall reconsider [the decision]." *Yomiuri shimbun,* December 5, 1988.

6. See *Yomiuri shimbun,* October 4, 28, 1991.

7. See *Yomiuri shimbun,* December 7, 1988.

8. Mark Manyin, "Breaking the Silence," 185.

9. *Yomiuri shimbun,* October 24, 1991, "Kanzeika no nami" no. 3.

10. *Asahi shimbun*, December 14, 1993.

11. Ibid.

12. Ibid.

13. Ibid. In another account, the Agriculture Ministry's stiff resistance was likened to the Imperial Army's readiness to fight to the last bullet and the last man and to the Japanese waiting, after the fall of Okinawa, for the A-bomb to be dropped on Hiroshima. Hitoshi Noguchi, "Kome sakokuron no kyoten: seijika to chihoshi" [Positions on (Japan) as a country closed to rice: politicians and local newspapers], *Shokun!* (January 1994): 138.

14. *Asahi shimbun*, December 14, 1993.

15. Ibid.

16. Ibid. On the softening of the Agriculture Ministry's position, see also *Asahi shimbun*, May 21, 1990. On the leading LDP power brokers on agriculture at that time, see the excellent treatment by Aurelia George, *Rice Politics in Japan*, Pacific Economic Papers no. 159 (Canberra: Australian National University, Research School of Pacific Studies, May 1988), 18–31.

17. *Asahi shimbun*, December 14, 1993.

18. Ibid.; interview with Charles J. O'Mara, May 16, 1996. O'Mara was the chief negotiator in the U.S. Department of Agriculture during the negotiations over Japanese rice imports.

19. *Asahi shimbun*, December 14, 1993.

20. Ibid.

21. *Asahi shimbun*, November 27, 1993.

22. O'Mara interview; Kensuke Karube, *Nichi-Bei kome kosho* [U.S.-Japan rice negotiations] (Tokyo: Chuo koron, 1997), 91–98; *Asahi shimbun*, December 14, 1993.

23. The formula was conceived by the Swiss (O'Mara interview; Karube, *Nichi-Bei kome kosho*, 132).

24. *Asahi shimbun*, December 14, 1993.

25. Ibid.; O'Mara interview.

26. *Asahi shimbun*, December 14, 1993.

27. Ibid.

28. Ibid.; O'Mara interview.

29. *Asahi shimbun*, October 23 and November 7, 1993.

30. *Asahi shimbun*, November 7, 1993.

31. Ibid.

32. *Asahi shimbun*, October 23, 1993.

33. Ibid.

34. *Asahi shimbun,* November 1, 1993.

35. *Asahi shimbun,* October 27, 1993.

36. *Asahi shimbun,* October 28, 1993.

37. *Asahi shimbun,* November 1, 1993.

38. Ibid.

39. *Asahi shimbun,* December 14, 1993.

40. Ibid.

41. Ibid.

42. *Asahi shimbun,* December 21, 1993.

43. The Japanese decision to import rice on an emergency basis had prompted some critics in Geneva to label Japan "self-serving" (*Asahi shimbun,* November 3, 1993). Earlier in 1993, in a speech in Brussels, Mickey Kantor had remarked: "Japan has not made a meaningful contribution to the Uruguay Round in three years"—a comment which prompted an ad hominem retort from the Foreign Ministry's Michihiko Kobayashi: "Kantor is a new boy who doesn't know the details of the negotiations" (*Asahi shimbun,* March 30, 1993). Dunkel's appraisal of Japan's multilateral performance, as reported in *Asahi shimbun,* November 1, 1993, is notable: "As a major trading country, Japan should have done better [in the Uruguay Round]."

3. THE FSX AIRCRAFT NEGOTIATIONS, 1985–89

1. See *Conflicting U.S. Objectives in Weapon System Codevelopment: The FS-X Case,* RAND Research Brief no. 20, August 1995 (accessed at www.rand.org/publications/RB/RB20.html).

2. James E. Auer, "FSX kosho wa ko shite ketchaku shita," *Chuo koron* (June 1990): 156–171.

3. Ibid.

4. The Toshiba scandal broke in 1987, when it was alleged that a subsidiary of the Japanese electronics firm Toshiba had supplied sensitive military hardware to the Soviet Union, angering the Reagan administration, which had long sought to restrict technology transfer to the Soviet bloc.

5. In late 1985 the U.S. Department of Commerce had decided to investigate charges that Japanese manufacturers, which dominated much of the U.S. market for computer chips, were illegally "dumping" their products in the United States.

6. Ryuichi Teshima, *Nippon FSX o ute* [The Japanese FSX] (Tokyo: Shincho sha, 1991), 41.

7. Soichiro Tahara, *Heisei Nihon no kanryo* [Japan's bureaucracy in the Heisei era] (Tokyo: Bungei shunju sha, 1990), 237.

8. Mark Lorell, *Troubled Partnership: A History of U.S.-Japan Collaboration on the FS-X Fighter* (Santa Monica, Calif.: RAND, 1995), 179, 189; Tahara, *Heisei Nihon no kanryo*, 242–243.

9. Teshima, *Nippon FSX o ute*, 78.

10. Ibid., 77.

11. See Shinji Otsuki, "The FSX Controversy Revived," *Japan Quarterly* 36 (October-December 1989): 433–443.

12. Teshima, *Nippon FSX o ute*, 81.

13. Ibid., 125.

14. Ibid., 129.

15. Ibid., 130.

16. Ibid., 142.

17. Ibid, 190.

18. Tahara, *Heisei Nihon no kanryo*, 249.

19. Teshima, *Nippon FSX o ute*, 191–192.

20. Ibid.

21. Lorell, *Troubled Partnership*, 75. Whether this was in fact Tokyo's intention is impossible to say with certainty. The Japanese strategy was "largely hidden from public view" (ibid.).

22. Tahara, *Heisei Nihon no kanryo*, 250.

23. Teshima, *Nippon FSX o ute*, 124.

24. Ibid., 79.

25. Auer, "FSX kosho wa ko shite ketchaku shita," 160.

26. Teshima, *Nippon FSX o ute*, 193, 195.

27. Ibid., 61–62.

28. Lorell, *Troubled Partnership*, 128.

29. Michael J. Green, *Arming Japan: Defense Production, Alliance Politics, and the Postwar Search for Autonomy* (New York: Columbia University Press, 1995), 96.

30. Tahara, *Heisei Nihon no kanryo*, 242–243.

31. Lorell, *Troubled Partnership*, 412.

32. Teshima, *Nippon FSX o ute*, 77, 73.

33. Ibid.

34. Green, *Arming Japan*, 156.

35. Tahara, *Heisei Nihon no kanryo*, 245; Teshima, *Nippon FSX o ute, 80.*

4. RENEGOTIATING THE U.S.-JAPAN SECURITY RELATIONSHIP, 1991–96

1. Admiral Sakuma continued in his role as an influential éminence grise after his retirement, and his influence was felt throughout the more direct negotiations from 1994 through 1997.

2. See Anne M. Dixon, "Can Eagles and Cranes Flock Together?" in *The U.S.-Japan Alliance: Past, Present, and Future*, ed. Michael J. Green and Patrick M. Cronin (New York: Council on Foreign Relations Press, 1999), 155, 156.

3. Patrick Cronin and Michael Green, *Redefining the U.S.-Japan Alliance: Tokyo's National Defense Program*, McNair Paper 31 (Washington, D.C.: National Defense University, November 1994), 2.

4. Ibid., 3.

5. This account of the crisis comes from the Federation of American Scientists Web site: http://www.fas.org/man/dod-101/ops/taiwan_strait.htm.

6. The Okinawan base negotiation would still linger six years later, however. This failure to resolve the issue owed much to the fact that, regarding the issue of Okinawan bases, Japanese and American negotiators had to cope with local municipal and national prefectural interests and Tokyo officials were reluctant to make public statements about national needs that would antagonize Okinawans.

CONCLUSIONS

1. Raymond Cohen, *Negotiating across Cultures: International Communication in an Interdependent World* (Washington, D.C.: United States Institute of Peace Press, 1997), 33–35.

2. Richard H. Solomon, *Chinese Negotiating Behavior: Pursuing Interests through "Old Friends"* (Washington, D.C.: United States Institute of Peace Press, 1999), xiv–xv.

3. Ruth Benedict, *The Chrysanthemum and the Sword: Patterns of Japanese Culture* (Rutland, Vt., and Tokyo: Charles E. Tuttle, 1946), 13.

GLOSSARY

The following terms are often used by Japanese negotiators or in reference to Japanese negotiating behavior.

amae sense of dependence

atomawashi postponement

banana takaki banana-slicing tactics

benkyokai study group

bokansha bystander

bubun kaiho partial (market) opening

chinmoku silence

chowateki bunka harmony-based culture

dakyo compromise

dameji kontororu damage control

gaiatsu foreign pressure

gaiko diplomacy

gaiko kosho diplomatic negotiations

ganbaru to make an effort

ganji garame tied up in knots

garasubari aboveboard

genjo iji status-quo

gibu ando teku give-and-take

giin gaiko politicians in diplomacy

gyosha trading firm

hado pancha hard puncher

hantai opposition

happo fusagari surrounded on all sides

happo yabure defenseless on all sides

haragei reading the opponent

higaisha ishiki victim's mentality

honne real intentions; real feelings

ichimai iwa monolith

iesu batto yes, but

iiwake excuse

ikkansei consistency

imeji appu improve one's image

ipponka unify (achieve consensus)

ippoteki unilateral; one-sided

ishin denshin tacit, unspoken understanding

ishisotsu understanding

jiko shucho self-promotion

jimujikan administrative vice minister

jiyuka liberalization (of domestic market)

jokyo handan to assess a situation

jokyo ni tekikaku ni taio dekiru the ability to respond to the situation correctly

josei conditions; situation

jumbi preparations

kao o tateru to save face

kento suru to study (a matter)

kesshin resolve

kiken kaihi crisis avoidance

kikikan sense of crisis

kiki kanri crisis management

kogen reishoku flatter with honeyed words

kojitsu excuse; pretext

kokusaika internationalization

kokusai koken international contribution

konsensasu consensus

koritsuka to become isolated

kurofune black ships

kyodo kaihatsu joint development

kyojakusei vulnerability

kyokumen dakai breakthrough

kyuchi ni ochiru to fall into dire straits

maemuki forward-looking

maruchi-bi bilateral in a multilateral framework

masatsu friction

meikakuka suru to clarify

mentsu face

minaosu reevaluation

motazaru kuni have-not country

nakama ishiki go-between mentality

nattoryoku persuasiveness

nawabara arasoi territorial squabbling

nawabari shugi bureaucratic territorialism

nemawashi building consensus before moving; prior consultation; testing the waters

Nihon kabushikigaisha Japan, Inc.

ningen kankei personal relations

nisha takuitsu two things; pick one

no tachi off-limits

oendan supporting delegation

ogori arrogance

omote surface; front

reigaiteki exceptional

rikutsu excuse

saigo no girigiri the last moment

saikento review

saishu dankai final stage

sakoku kanjo closed-country mentality

sei i sincerity

seikei bunri separating politics from economics

sekininkan sense of responsibility

senkensei foresight

sensei teacher

shimaguni island country

shingikan councilor

shin-i true intentions

shokku shock

sogoshugi reciprocity

soron sansei, kakuron hantai agree in principle; disagree on details

soto outside; foreign

tai-Bei tsuizui gaiko diplomacy of following the United States

taisei conditions; situation

taisei juno shugi situational ethic

tamamushiiro iridescent

tatemae superficial opinion

teishisei low-profile

tekiosei adaptability; flexibility

tokushu special; exceptional

torihiki ryoku bargaining skill

uchi inside; not foreign

ura behind-the-scenes

wa harmony

yakusoku promise; pledge

yamu o ezu unavoidable; inevitable

yumoa no sensu sense of humor

yuyo postponement; delay

zempoi gaiko multidirectional diplomacy

zenryoku o tsukusu to exhaust all efforts

zettai hantai absolute opposition

zoku (policy) tribe or tribes

ABOUT THE AUTHORS

Michael Blaker is a fellow at the East Asian Studies Center, University of Southern California, specializing in Japanese domestic politics, Japanese diplomacy, and U.S.-Japan relations. He has taught at Columbia University (where he also earned his doctorate), USC, the Fletcher School of Law and Diplomacy, and, most recently, Harvard University, where he was senior research associate in the program on U.S.-Japan relations. An Abe Fellow (1993–94), he was the initial holder of the Japan chair at the Center for Strategic and International Studies in Washington, D.C., director of the project on U.S.-Japan relations in multilateral organizations at Columbia, director of the U.S.-Japan parallel studies project at UNA-USA, and distinguished professor at Nihon University during 1983. His published work includes *Japanese International Negotiating Style, Japan at the Polls, The Politics of Trade*, and many journal articles in Japanese and English on Japanese foreign relations and Japanese-American relations.

Paul Giarra is a senior analyst responsible for the Strategic Assessment Center's Office of Global Strategies at Science Applications International Corporation. He supervises and conducts long-range planning and strategic assessments of regional political, economic, technological, energy, and security trends for domestic and international government and commercial clients; he also leads analysis of future U.S. defense technologies and weapons systems. During his twenty-four-year career as a naval aviator, naval strategic planner, and political-military strategic planner for Far East, South Asia, and Pacific issues, Giarra served in two ships, in two P-3 squadrons, on two major staffs, and attended two war colleges. On the Navy Staff, he was involved in reorienting Navy strategic and programmatic priorities at the end of the Cold War. During his final Navy assignment, he served for almost five years as the senior country director for Japan on the staff of the Secretary of Defense.

Giarra is a graduate of Harvard College, has a master's degree in international relations from Salve Regina College, graduated with highest distinction from the U.S. Naval War College's Command and Staff course, and attended the U.S. National War College–equivalent Japanese National Institute of Defense Studies.

Ezra Vogel is the Henry Ford II Research Professor at Harvard University, where he earned his doctorate in sociology and where he taught from the 1960s until 2000. He has been director of Harvard's East Asian Research Center, chairman of the Council for East Asian Studies, director (and subsequently honorary director) of the program on U.S.-Japan relations at the Center for International Affairs, director of the Fairbank Center, and the first director of the Asia Center.

Vogel has researched and lectured extensively in Japan and China, and is the author of many books, including *Japan's New Middle Class, Canton under Communism, Comeback, One Step Ahead in China: Guangdong under Reform, The Four Little Dragons: The Spread of Industrialization in East Asia,* and *Japan as Number One: Lessons for America* (which is the best-selling nonfiction book in Japan by a Western author). Most recently he has published *Is Japan Still Number One?*

From fall 1993 to fall 1995, Vogel took a two-year leave of absence from Harvard to serve as the national intelligence officer for East Asia at the National Intelligence Council in Washington, D.C. He directed the American Assembly on China in November 1996 and the Joint Chinese-American Assembly between China and the United States in 1998.

Patrick Cronin is assistant administrator responsible for policy and budget at the United States Agency for International Development. His previous positions include director of research and studies at the United States Institute of Peace, and deputy director and director of research at the Institute for National Strategic Studies at the National Defense University. Cronin earned his M.Phil. and D.Phil. degrees at the University of Oxford and has taught at both the Paul H. Nitze School for Advanced International Studies at Johns Hopkins University and the University of Virginia. His numerous publications include *The U.S.-Japan Alliance: Past, Present, and Future,* of which he was coeditor and coauthor and which was published by the Council on Foreign Relations in 1999.